The Unknown Leader

TO MY PARENTS:

They keep giving and I keep taking,
both of us nourished
by the endless abundance of
the urge to love and be loved.
This is the home that started me off
on the path to self-discovery…

HUSSEIN A AL-BANAWI

The Unknown Leader

DISCOVER THE LEADER IN YOU

KoganPage

LONDON PHILADELPHIA NEW DELHI

Part One

Responding to your personal leadership challenge

Discovering the Unknown Leader

Our world has many leaders who are obvious and widely acclaimed – captains of industry, high-achieving academics, CEOs, heads of state, dignitaries, philanthropists, entertainers, champion athletes. Their pictures appear on our television screens, newspaper front pages, internet sites and magazine covers. But our world also depends on leaders who are not so obvious. They are all around us, filling crucial roles at every level of society, in all kinds of organizations and communities. They've achieved extraordinary work that may not receive much publicity and that sometimes takes a long time to come to fruition. Some serve as mentors to others who may become well known in their own right while the mentors themselves remain obscure. Others work quietly behind the scenes, scarcely noticed even as they make everyone around them better.

These are the Unknown Leaders – role models from all walks of life, at all levels in our society and within our countless organizations and institutions. They deserve just as much recognition as the famous ones.

I've made it a mission of mine to celebrate the Unknown Leaders among us and to pay tribute to Unknown Leaders everywhere, with the hope of inspiring you to become one.

In this book, I'll attempt to shed light on what makes a true leader, offering some insights and ideas for those who aspire to join the next generation of leaders, in the Middle East and around the world. I'll also describe a new model of leadership – leadership that is not about chasing fame or glory but about contributing to a better society; not about accumulating wealth but about living a satisfying life; not about winning every contest but about venturing and taking risks in pursuit of excellence. It's a model of leadership that is relevant to people everywhere – including you.

I'll begin with three examples of Unknown Leaders – three among many whom I could have chosen. You may never have heard of any of the three people I'll profile in the next few pages. Their faces may never appear on the cover of a magazine or on a television programme. They are not CEOs of corporations, statesmen, celebrities or medal-winning athletes. Yet each is a leader with powerful vision who has done a lot to make our world a better place – and, God willing, will do still more in the years to come. They are Unknown Leaders I have come to admire deeply, and examples of the kind of quiet heroism our world badly needs.

DR WALEED BUKHARI
The nerves of a fighter pilot, the soul of a surgeon

Dr Waleed Bukhari is one of the world's most highly qualified laparoscopic surgeons. I am proud to say that he is also a close personal friend.

I first met Waleed through a distant family relationship that dates back almost 20 years. I was very close to his father as well, a retired fighter pilot in the Saudi Air Force who was really a great human being – a man with a deep and fervent belief in the future as a time of opportunity, hope and positive change. It's easy to see how this belief has influenced and shaped his son's views and values.

When I got to know Waleed, the two of us discovered an instant emotional and intellectual affinity. Over time, that natural chemistry between us grew stronger and stronger, blossoming into a sense of shared values and deep-rooted respect. We've shared our personal views on the most important topics, sought one another's advice on family-related matters, and developed great mutual trust in one another's judgement.

A few years back, when my father was ailing, I asked Dr Waleed's advice about obtaining the best medical care for him. After offering some wise counsel, Dr Waleed added, 'By the way, I'll be with you as you tackle these challenges. I'm taking time off from my work to be there for you.' It was a remarkably selfless and generous act. In the days that followed, Dr Waleed supported me emotionally and helped me engage with my father's doctors until he recovered safely – and Dr Waleed's help in making difficult decisions throughout the period was invaluable to me and helped us grow even closer. It is times like this that reveal the true face of an individual.

Dr Waleed Bukhari's medical talents are extraordinary and widely recognized. He has saved the lives of hundreds of patients through the knowledge in his brain and the skill in his hands, and he has enhanced the quality of life for thousands of others. Yet his path to this career of leadership in one of today's most demanding professions was not a simple or straightforward one.

Born in Saudi Arabia in 1958, young Waleed grew up wanting to be a fighter pilot like his father, who had flown heroic missions for the Saudi Air Force during the 1967 war. For Waleed, his handsome father was a romantic figure, especially when he donned his helmet and flight suit. But he strongly suspected that his father didn't want him to follow in his footsteps. Nonetheless, after graduating from high school, Waleed secretly applied to the Air Force Academy in Riyadh, hoping to keep his father in the dark about his plans.

Waleed's scheme fell apart when the director of the school sent a telex message to his father, who was in fact an old friend: 'Congratulations! We've admitted your son.' Waleed's father was furious. He took Waleed aside and explained why he did not want him to become an air force pilot. 'Waleed, you're my only son. I was one of six children, and joining the air force was the only way I could support my family. But you have other options, and I will not allow my only son to risk his life in battle.'

Waleed was even more surprised at what his father went on to say. 'You know, fighting and killing people was not my first choice. I don't believe in it. Nothing except immediate self-defence can justify killing people. It's not something I want a child of mine to do.'

'Take a couple of years off', Waleed's father concluded. 'Get a back-pack; see the world; explore. Figure out what you want to do. I'll support you – but, whatever you do, don't choose to be a fighter pilot.'

Not until years later, when Waleed had become a successful surgeon and had children of his own, did the two men have a heart-to-heart talk in which Waleed's father admitted that, as a boy, he had always dreamed of being a physician himself.

That summer after high school, Waleed made plans for a round-the-world trip, taking advantage of his father's generous offer. One hot day ('You could fry an egg on the bonnet of a car', he recalls), Waleed was driving around Jeddah when he saw a banner advertising the imminent opening of the King Faisal Medical School. He also spotted a bunch of men, all dressed in simple working clothes, wearing paper face masks over their mouths and noses, and sweating profusely. They were carrying plastic-wrapped bags that were unmistakably in the size and shape of human bodies into one of the nearby buildings.

Intrigued, Waleed went over to one of the workmen and asked, 'Can I help?' It turned out that they were delivering cadavers for use in research in the new medical school, and the workmen gratefully accepted Waleed's help.

After a few minutes, one of the men working there came over to Waleed and said, 'Young man, you have to become a doctor.'

Waleed was surprised. 'Why?' he asked.

The stranger replied, 'Because we've had six men faint from the smell of the cadavers, but it doesn't seem to bother you at all – and you're not even wearing a face mask.' Then he introduced himself. 'I'm Tuki Tuki, and I'm the first dean of the new medical school.'

This chance encounter changed Waleed Bukhari's life. He decided then and there to give medical school a try. He applied for admission, was accepted, and began his studies that autumn – much to his father's delight.

Medical school had its ups and downs. During the second year, Waleed took the required anatomy course, one of the most demanding in the curriculum, and found himself growing increasingly impatient. 'I hated sitting in a chair, reading thick books', Dr Waleed recalls. 'I wanted to be outside, doing exciting, dangerous things. I had learned to scuba-dive when I was 14. I liked desert camping with no radio and no compass, like a real Bedouin. I liked hiking, taking long drives.' Waleed still has a strong adventurous streak. He rides motorcycles, enjoys drag-racing fast cars on deserted back streets, and has learned to skydive. No wonder this adventurous young man began to chafe at the rigours of medical school.

Waleed began to toy with the idea of leaving medical school. His father left the decision completely up to him. But one of Waleed's professors, a much-published world authority on oncology named Izdeen Abraham, would hear nothing of it. 'You're going to be a great doctor', he told Waleed. 'You're brilliant. Just plant yourself in the chair and read! That's all you have to do to be an outstanding success.'

Waleed took his advice. He remained on his course, became one of the first graduates of the King Faisal Medical School, and developed a lifelong friendship with Dr Izdeen – in fact, they still play racquetball together on occasion.

It was during an internship after graduation that Dr Waleed discovered how much he loved surgery. A resident surgeon allowed Dr Waleed to do a simple hernia operation. The delicate manual artistry of surgery immediately appealed to him, reminding him of sketching and painting, two crafts he had always loved. And of course the high-stakes challenges involving human life in surgery appealed to his personality. Dr Waleed was hooked for life. 'From that point on,' he says, 'my work was my passion.'

Dr Waleed soon discovered that he had the talent, attitude and intelligence to become a world-class surgeon. What he may not have realized was that he was also gifted with powerful leadership abilities. These had the opportunity to surface in 1989 after Dr Waleed attended a medical conference on colon cancer in Monterey, California:

> *I was coming back to my hotel room at two o'clock one afternoon at the end of a long meeting. I wanted to take a rest for half an hour and just relax a bit, when I passed by a darkened room with a half-open door. Inside I could see people watching an eight-millimetre movie. So I just pushed the door open and went in, and there was a French surgeon, speaking to a small group of doctors from around the world. He was presenting the first-ever film made showing a cholecystectomy – a gall bladder removal – using the endoscopic technique. I was amazed by the film and by how he described the process.*

When Dr Waleed returned home to Saudi Arabia, one of his medical colleagues asked him, 'So what are the Americans doing that's different from us when it comes to colon cancer?'

Dr Waleed replied, 'Absolutely nothing. But the French are doing something unbelievable called laparoscopic surgery. They remove the gall bladder through a tiny incision, and the very next day the patient can sit up in bed, eat a meal and leave the hospital.' (At the time, standard practice called for a week of intravenous feeding and a two-week hospital stay after a gall bladder operation.)

Dr Waleed knew right away that it was his mission to learn laparoscopic surgery and to bring this revolutionary new technique to the Middle East. He spent the next five years making it happen. In the process, he transformed himself from simply being a fine surgeon into being an innovative leader, educator and institution-builder in the world of Saudi medicine.

Within a few weeks, Dr Waleed was in Germany, studying laparoscopic surgery from some of the world's leading experts. 'I did my first operation – removing the colon from a pig – using very primitive equipment', he recalls. But it worked – and Dr Waleed now had the knowledge to bring this state-of-the-art medical method to his homeland.

However, when he tried to bring the technique to Saudi Arabia, the leading national university refused his offer, calling it 'nonsense'. Many physicians would have given up, and perhaps moved their practice overseas. But instead Dr Waleed contacted a small private hospital just across the street from the university and offered to set up a laparoscopy team there.

The little hospital became a beehive of activity. 'We did 42 gall bladder surgeries in five days. We were working from morning until evening', Dr Waleed says.

The pace was fantastic, and the people at the university heard about it – along with the whole country. Our work became a big story in the news, and soon officials from King Abdulaziz University in Jeddah were on the phone, asking, 'Can we invite you to come and do these operations in our university?' We answered, 'Of course!' And soon we were training all the assistant professors, associate professors and professors.

In 1992, at the tender age of 32, Dr Waleed became director of a small, 100-bed hospital in Jeddah where he began performing 600 laparoscopic operations a year. During his tenure there, the national minister of health visited the hospital for the very first time. In the middle of his tour, the minister approached Dr Waleed and said, 'I didn't really come here to see the hospital – I came to see you. Talk to me about this new type of surgery.'

Impressed by what he learned, the minister arranged a government grant of 72 million riyals to refurbish the hospital, enlarge it, and transform it into one of the best small hospitals in Jeddah. Soon Dr Waleed himself was transferred to a much bigger, 1,600-bed hospital, and named chairman of the Prince Sultan Center for Advanced Laparoscopic Surgeries.

The new post, and the widespread recognition of the value of laparo-scopy, gave Dr Waleed the opportunity he'd been waiting for to revolutionize surgery in Saudi Arabia. 'I planned and executed the first international conference on laparoscopy in the Middle East', he recalls. But organizing such a programme wasn't easy. In fact, it called forth an entirely new set of leadership skills from the young physician.

At first, Dr Waleed hoped to secure government funding in support of the conference. But the global recession of the early 1990s was in full swing, and money was in short supply. The health minister told Dr Waleed simply, 'God bless you, but we cannot help.' Disappointed, Dr Waleed vowed to find the necessary resources elsewhere.

Dr Waleed spent months visiting prominent businessmen and philanthropists throughout Saudi Arabia. He educated them about the importance of this new surgical technique, excited them about the international prestige the conference would bring to the country, and cajoled them to support the programme from their own pockets. One by one, they were captivated by his passion and eloquence.

One company head donated $50,000 in start-up funds. A second pledged $100,000 and promised to use his influence to generate newspaper coverage of the event. A third offered to pay for a banquet for all attendees at the conference. The director of Saudi Airlines promised to provide free tickets for professors travelling from Washington, Rio de Janeiro and other cities around the globe. And with momentum clearly building for the conference, the government finally came through with a donation of help from the Ministry of Youth, including access to the facilities of King Fahd City and a pro bono presentation by one of the Kingdom's most famous traditional dance groups to entertain the visiting dignitaries.

In the end, Dr Waleed's resourcefulness and zeal made the long-shot conference into an enormous success. 'We attracted 32 international speakers from America, Europe and South America, along with over 1,000 attendees from around the world', he says. And the conference put Saudi Arabian hospitals and universities, along with Dr Waleed himself, on the global health care map. It created contacts with leading medical institutions and world-class experts from the United States and Europe to Russia and Singapore, all of which have proven invaluable in the continuing growth, advancement and improvement of high-tech medical care in Saudi Arabia in the subsequent decades.

Dr Waleed's leadership abilities came to the forefront in his venturesome work to bring laparoscopy to the Middle East, but he also expresses those leadership traits in the operating room every day.

Surgery, Dr Waleed emphasizes, is a team sport. 'It's not just the surgeon who makes the difference', he says. 'It's the surgeon, the endocrinologist, the cardiologist, the psychologist, the nutritionist, the bariatrician, the physiotherapist and the exercise trainer. They make up the team that translates to a successful outcome and a healthier patient.'

Of course, every team must have a captain, and in the operating theatre it is the surgeon who leads. 'Unfortunately,' says Dr Waleed with a smile, 'I am the lead performer, whether I like it or not. It's not because I want to be a star. I believe in loyalty above all, because loyalty enhances the team spirit, and makes the difference between a successful team and a fragile, easy-to-collapse team. Disloyalty can break the team and dismantle it.'

He is quick to explain:

> Disloyalty does not mean leaving our hospital to go and work somewhere else. It means failing to play your part as a true partner. As partners, we have to take care of one another's interests. I would cut myself open if necessary to protect my partners' interests, and I expect no less from them. So if you are a person who thinks only of himself, and shows no concern about the burden of work that others take, or fails to act to protect the reputation of his partners, then that is disloyalty – and it shatters the sense of partnership that is essential to successful medicine.

Self-centred motives have no place in Dr Waleed's code of values.

As leader of the team, Dr Waleed takes ultimate responsibility for the atmosphere in the operating room. 'Negativity on the part of one person can reflect on everyone else, and lead to unnecessary complications', he says.

> I have to combat this with a positive spirit. A cheerful smile can make a big difference. So does being efficient and fast. I have the fastest surgical team in the country, and I don't mind bragging about it! On a given morning, I usually

*work with four teams in four rooms at once, moving
from one to the next – hop, hop, hop, hop, hop, hop – up to
12 patients a day, in a 12-hour span.*

The energy demanded by this schedule is enormous. Dr Waleed usually doesn't stop to eat or take a rest during these marathon surgery sessions, except perhaps for a coffee and a quick bite. He learned from one of his teachers – John Fong, a talented liver transplant surgeon from Pittsburgh – how to catnap for up to 20 minutes while in the midst of his intense working schedule (while standing up, if necessary). After this kind of brief rest, he is refreshed and ready to keep working for several more hours.

Faith is Dr Waleed's other source of internal energy. 'I believe that Islam sustains my work and helps produce the results I've been blessed with', he says.

Whatever the sources of Dr Waleed Bukhari's intellectual, spiritual, physical and emotional strength, they have produced, and are producing, enormous benefits for his many patients as well as for the medical students, physicians and many other professionals whose work has been guided and enriched by his teaching. Dr Waleed's face may never appear on the cover of a magazine; he will never be a high-profile politician, a corporate CEO or a global celebrity. But his quiet leadership is helping to transform the practice of medicine in the Middle East and around the world, saving and improving countless lives in the process.

Dr Waleed's story illustrates how Unknown Leaders can emerge in unlikely circumstances. At times, the call for leadership comes to the surface when the odds are against you and the battle is an uphill fight. In Dr Waleed's case, his youthful talent came to fruition at a time when external resources were scarce. It would have been easy for him to become discouraged and give up on his dream of making Saudi Arabia among the world leaders in laparoscopic surgery. Instead, he responded with energy and creativity to the call to leadership. The result has been a lasting impact on the lives of many in decades past and for years to come through Dr Waleed's pioneering contributions.

DR ASMA SIDDIKI
Bringing the gift of culture to a new generation

Some Unknown Leaders have an impact that is national or regional in scope. As we've seen, Dr Waleed Bukhari is helping to change the face of Saudi medicine, making his homeland a global leader in his field.

Other Unknown Leaders, no less worthy, pursue personal visions that may appear, at first glance, less ambitious. But these leaders often touch lives in ways that are just as profound, leaving a beneficial impact that only grows with time. Consider, for example, the remarkable vision now being developed by Dr Asma Siddiki, an energetic and creative young woman whose intelligence and thoughtfulness I greatly admire.

When I first met Asma Siddiki, she was an associate dean and the director for degree programmes at the Dubai School of Government (DSG), an important regional educational institute established in 2005.

At the time of our first acquaintance, I had no personal connection with DSG. However, one of Dr Asma's roles was to develop partnerships with individuals and organizations that could support DSG in its mission. Having heard of my personal interest in and commitment to the development of leadership talent for the Middle East region, Dr Asma decided that I could be a useful contributor to DSG's efforts, and so she set about 'wooing' me on the school's behalf – cordially, respectfully and very persistently! She would visit me at my offices in Jeddah and keep me informed about the latest new programmes and projects at DSG, asking my advice about new initiatives and conveying her passionate belief in the school and its value to the region.

I was so impressed by Dr Asma's professionalism, commitment and communication skills that, after a few meetings, I decided that DSG and our company, Banawi Industrial Group (B.I.G.), should form a close association. We had been developing a plan to expand our corporate social responsibility (CSR) programme, and we had realized that we could benefit from the advice and guidance of an outside organization with expertise in analysing social challenges – particularly in the area of enterprise leadership development, our special focus. (I explain more about our CSR initiative in Chapter 8.) I invited Dr Asma to get DSG involved in helping us. She quickly grasped the concept and responded with enthusiasm, selling the idea to her colleagues and connecting us with leading experts on the DSG faculty. The programme she helped create proved to be beneficial and rewarding for both organizations. The remarkable job that Dr Asma did on this project confirmed for me that she is an outstanding talent and a remarkable example of an Unknown Leader in action.

Over time, I've learned more about Dr Asma and her impressive personal story. She has been an innovative educational leader for more than a decade. She started her career as an administrator at Effat University, the first private women's university in Saudi Arabia, where she rose to become vice-dean, developing and implementing enrolment management, recruitment, and retention plans that helped put the institution on a sound business footing. She also helped to create a cross-curriculum student development programme that greatly enriched the educational experience of thousands of young female students.

Later, at DSG, in addition to working with outside corporate associates like B.I.G., Dr Asma established connections with other
universities throughout the region and the world, arranging to bring
top-flight academic experts from Europe, Asia and North America
to teach and lecture at the school. She also spearheaded the school's
efforts to earn licensing and accreditation for its master's degree
programme from the United Arab Emirates Ministry of Higher
Education.

After three years at DSG, Dr Asma joined an international consulting
firm that specializes in helping colleges and universities improve
their own management systems. Based in Dubai, Dr Asma travels
throughout the Middle East to work with college presidents, deans,
regents and boards of trustees to help them solve difficult leadership
challenges. Her successful track record as a university administrator
gives her the experience, knowledge and credibility needed to fulfil
this advisory role very effectively.

However, what drives Dr Asma most in her life is something quite
separate from her work in consulting. Heritage Summers is a programme Dr Asma has developed that brings young people, aged
16 and older, to Cambridge university in England. The students,
who originate from countries around the greater Middle East region
but also from other parts of the world, spend a summer taking
a variety of college-level courses, studying such standard subjects
as science, mathematics and languages but also being immersed
in the culture, history, geography and economics of the Muslim
world.

At first, the concept seems counter-intuitive. Why take young people
from countries like Jordan, Saudi Arabia and the Emirates to the
United Kingdom in order to learn more about their own cultural
heritage? Couldn't they learn about subjects like classic Persian
literature, the pioneering anthropological studies of Al-Biruni, and
the economic and cultural impact of the spice trade on the Middle
East – all topics that will be included in the Heritage Summers

curriculum – without leaving their home region? Of course they could. But Dr Asma – who earned her own master's and PhD degrees at Oxford – is a believer in the special value of studying one's own heritage against a broader global background and experiencing the culture of learning at a truly global institution.

Dr Asma says:

> *In our part of the world there is sometimes a feeling of defensiveness about the riches of Middle Eastern culture – especially given the history of conflict between the West and East. So when young students learn about our history, literature, art or science in school in the region, it often comes across as propaganda or indoctrination. These topics are often presented in a one-sided fashion, with criticism obscured or forbidden – as if it's unacceptable to think that anything we've ever done in our part of the world has been less than perfect. Paradoxically, but understandably, this elimination of questioning makes students dubious or even cynical about the reality of what they are hearing.*

> *For this reason it can mean more for a young Arab to hear a lecture about the golden age of Arab culture from a PhD student at Oxford – who may well be a non-Arab himself. In that setting, you know that what you are hearing is not propaganda, but the truth as uncovered by scholars, based on serious, world-class research. And it also means you feel free to talk openly about our history, our culture, and its strengths and weaknesses. Criticism can be absorbed, understood and argued about once it is removed from the defensive 'us against them' context in which it is usually discussed. The result is a deeper understanding and appreciation of our cultural heritage – something our young people really need in order to participate fully in the global world of today.*

Heritage Summers was launched as a pilot programme in 2011 with nine students from throughout the Middle East–North Africa (MENA) region as well as Pakistan, the United States and France. They heard talks from eminent lecturers such as Professor Yasir Suleiman, professor of modern Arabic studies and director of the Centre for Islamic Studies at Cambridge, and Caroline Montagu, Countess of Sandwich, a Cambridge graduate, trustee of the Saudi British Society and member of the Saudi British Business Council. They studied with tutors from a wide range of backgrounds – some who are Muslim scholars from Middle Eastern nations, and others from North America or Europe who are fascinated by learning about this part of the world. They came away from the experience with both a deeper knowledge of themselves and a more rounded understanding of the world into which they were born.

Excited by the initial success of Heritage Summers, Dr Asma has big plans for the future. She eventually hopes to broaden and institutionalize the programme under the banner of Alpha1 Education, to include Heritage Winters – which will bring students from around the world to centres of learning in the Arab world during the semester breaks of December and January – and Heritage Retreats, which will offer adult learners the opportunity to delve more deeply into a cultural inheritance they may never have fully examined. Dr Asma's modest programme may some day blossom into a major programme that will touch the lives of hundreds or even thousands of individuals.

Asma Siddiki illustrates many of the traits of the Unknown Leader. She is an innovative thinker, one with the gift of repeatedly recognizing unfulfilled needs and the creativity to devise unique new programmes to meet those needs. She is a high-energy, self-disciplined manager, with the patience and persistence to organize the hundreds of small but important details that go into making any complex project a value proposition. Perhaps most impressively, she has shown the ability to create a powerfully inspiring vision and communicate that vision to other people, winning their enthusiastic support in making it a reality.

Look beneath the surface of any truly innovative new product, service or programme, and you will find an Unknown Leader like Asma Siddiki at work!

DR GHAZI BINZAGR
The balance between business and the human sciences

Dr Ghazi Binzagr is a member of the Binzagr family business, which started as a trading company in the Arabian peninsula more than one hundred and thirty years ago. He serves his family business in various executive capacities. He is also deeply involved in the life of his community, participating actively in such organizations as the Jeddah Economic Forum and the Jeddah Chamber of Commerce and Industry, as well as serving on the Honorary Board of Advisors of Effat University, the first non-profit private institution of higher education for women in Saudi Arabia.

I first met Dr Ghazi when we served together on a think tank headed by the then governor of Saudi Arabia's Madinah region. This was an unusual group of business people and others who were happy and honoured to respond to the call to serve – partly because of our shared commitment to a part of our country with special spiritual significance as the resting place of the Prophet Mohammed (Peace Be Upon Him), partly because of our respect for HRH Prince Migrin bin Abdulaziz Al Saud himself, who exemplified many of the finest traits of leadership. The result was a stimulating series of meetings and in-depth deliberations.

The way in which the think tank meetings were conducted was also unusual – a powerful blend of professionalism and confidentiality that encouraged free and open discussion with little emotion but with high regard for sensitive issues.

I quickly discovered that Dr Ghazi was a first-class thinker with a gift for highlighting the 'soft' issues confronting the think tank, thereby complementing the others around the table with special knowledge of such 'hard' issues as infrastructure, the economy, finances, legal and regulatory concerns, and so on. Over time, Dr Ghazi and I began regularly challenging one another in discussions – not for the sake of needless argument but to allow every argument to be presented fully, without prejudgement. This helped produce a stimulating series of meetings and in-depth deliberations that made it possible for the think tank to emerge with a vision, a strategy and a 10-year plan for the region that was unique and a model for future private–public sector partnerships.

My experience on this task force with Dr Ghazi taught me some important lessons about working collaboratively with others. We often tend to prejudge arguments that are unfamiliar, rejecting good ideas without adequate consideration. I learned how important it is to be persistent when offering a new approach to a problem or an opportunity and, rather than giving up at the first sign of opposition, to present the idea again using a different perspective, a new example and a new angle, as well as plugging the gaps in your argument in response to the concerns brought forward by others. Often people gradually warm to a novel concept and begin to recognize its merits – not the first time it is described, but the second, third or fourth time.

Having enjoyed the opportunity to work with Dr Ghazi on the think tank, I made a point of getting to know him better in subsequent years. I discovered that Dr Ghazi's business accomplishments are very impressive – but more remarkable is the unusual story that lies behind them.

Although he represents the fourth generation of his family to participate in what he calls the 'merchant culture' of the Middle East, Dr Ghazi's personal passion was not to work in trade, sales or administration. As a young student, he'd become fascinated by the sciences, and as a result he majored in physics at the University of California in Santa Barbara. He then went to Thunderbird University in the United States at the request of his family to learn skills relevant to their business. An elective course he took there helped him discover the science of human behaviour within organizations and realize that his deepest wish was to devote himself to studying this complex, arcane topic at a high level.

Young Ghazi was conflicted to find himself drawn to the mental discipline of the sciences, which seemed far removed from the practical skills traditionally valued in the merchant culture from which he'd sprung. He was delighted one day to reread in the Holy Qu'ran a familiar verse that created a bridge between the physical sciences and the social sciences: 'We will show you Our signs on the horizon and within themselves, until it becomes clear to you that this is the truth; is it not enough that God is a Witness unto all these?' (Qu'ran 41:53). In these words, Ghazi heard the voice of God declaring that the truths hidden in the mysteries of earthly existence – the 'signs on the horizon and within [our]selves' – were also emblems and embodiments of divine truth. Science, then, could be a noble, even sacred, profession – one worthy of a lifetime's study. Ghazi saw that he could be a scientist and still focus on a field close to his family obligations.

Still, his desire to be a scientist created a quandary for young Ghazi. It had always been understood that he would apply his talents to working in the family business, which focused on trading and distributing fast-moving consumer goods, often representing major global corporations such as Unilever. He had followed family tradition in working at entry-level jobs at companies that were partners of his family business – for example, carrying boxes in a warehouse of the Randalls supermarket chain in Houston, Texas – but, after having a taste of business life, Ghazi now wanted to continue his academic studies by pursuing a PhD in the burgeoning field of organizational dynamics (OD). This created the concrete possibility of pursuing work in a field that would bridge science and practice.

He worried about what the reaction of his family would be. His father was supportive, but he didn't fully understand his son's interest, which created a somewhat painful dilemma for Ghazi. 'Go and study what you like', his father said. 'When you finish your degree, come back and we'll find a place for you in the family business.' The hard decision – how to reconcile Ghazi's scholarly interests and the demands of the family enterprise – would be postponed, but not eliminated.

Ghazi's years of studying OD were as fascinating as he'd hoped. He delved into philosophy, psychology, social theory and cultural anthropology, which opened his eyes to remarkable fields of knowledge that could be applied to improving the human condition.

Excited by what he had learned, and equipped with his newly minted PhD in organizational dynamics, Dr Ghazi returned home. He was hoping to find ways of applying his insights to understanding and influencing organizational systems starting with his own family's business. But at first he was disappointed. Not only did the company have no real application for the knowledge of a young PhD, but in general he found it was a huge challenge to explain his field to others within and around the business. 'What is this OD you keep talking about?' they would ask. 'Is it human resources?' Dr Ghazi struggled unsuccessfully to find a way to explain it. Meanwhile, he was required to do detailed managerial work that was a million miles from the world of science he'd become engrossed in.

This time of frustration was transformed into a turning point in Dr Ghazi's career thanks to a book he read – *The Work We Were Born to Do*, by Nick Williams. 'It's a book on career planning,' Dr Ghazi explains, 'but the author writes it philosophically. The author brings in philosophical ideas from Zen and Confucius, Islam and Sufism and Christianity, and takes you on a spiritual exploration that leads to what you are supposed to do in your life.'

Of course, the problem for Dr Ghazi was that 'the work he was born to do' seemed unrelated to the work he *had* to do for the family business. But the author had a practical suggestion for handling this dilemma. 'Having realized that you're something other than what you are packaged to do,' Dr Ghazi says, 'the author explains that it's foolish to just walk away from your current work. You have moral and financial obligations towards your family and towards yourself. To abandon all that would be reckless. So what he recommended was starting to express yourself in a parallel path as a volunteer. That idea opened the world for me.'

In the second half of the 1990s, Dr Ghazi began a new phase of his personal journey of self-discovery – a path of volunteer work, while remaining a manager in the family business, that would ultimately lead to a satisfying and rewarding resolution of his personal career dilemma.

The first volunteer project arose when managers in the family business were asked by the government's labour ministry to provide summer employment for senior students of the local commercial high school in Jeddah. These young people had good intentions, but their job qualifications were less than desired and their knowledge of the business world was limited. Knowing Dr Ghazi's interest in 'people problems', the leaders of the business asked him to tackle this issue – and Dr Ghazi tackled it as an intellectual, scientific and practical challenge. He worked with representatives of the government and of other family businesses to create a committee that developed an evaluation system to channel graduates into appropriate jobs where they would have the best chance of success.

Soon other projects arose, each representing the area where human development, community economic growth and business interests come together. Little by little, Dr Ghazi's wide-ranging interests and connections in the world of social science became known throughout Saudi society. He found himself being approached more and more often with requests for help with projects designed to enhance human skills and direct them into the most productive channels for the future of society. Soon Dr Ghazi had to become quite selective, choosing from among the available projects those with the greatest potential for transforming the region. All of this was on a volunteer, part-time basis, while Dr Ghazi continued to help manage the retail arm of his family's business.

Eventually, even managers from other parts of the family business heard about Dr Ghazi's work and began to approach him for advice regarding their own human capital challenges. It led to the next step in Dr Ghazi's journey – the formation of his own company, Wisaal Development Centre.

Wisaal applies knowledge from Dr Ghazi's academic training to the challenges of business and economic growth. For example, Wisaal recently managed a pilot training programme for 15 managers from the business, who studied modern techniques for work effectiveness, management effectiveness, and communications from experts in Singapore. Why Singapore? Because, as Dr Ghazi explains, Singapore represents a thriving city-state based on a holistic, tripartite model of development involving a close partnership among government, employers and labour that is both idealistic and pragmatic as well as action focused. This is a model that is very relevant to the challenges now facing Saudi society. Wisaal has plans to expand the pilot programme to include much more interaction between enterprise leaders from the two regions, increasing the knowledge and understanding of both.

Ghazi Binzagr's journey has been an unusual one – but he is very excited about the direction it has taken and gratified by the opportunities it has created for him. 'I now feel I have come full circle', he says.

> I am still a merchant, still doing what generations before
> me did and honouring who I am, but in a form that is
> designed for the 21st century. My ancestors imported
> products from the outside world – like a simple bar of soap
> – and brought value to our region by selling those products

*for the use of people here. Now I am doing the same thing,
except that the 'product' is human knowledge and ideas
about human and community development. I am bringing
these ideas from the outside world into our country and
blending them with our own ancient ways of wisdom to
create something that is uniquely ours yet relevant to our
modern world and to the global challenges of our time.*

Perhaps the most significant lesson that young people can take from
the career of Ghazi Binzagr is that choosing a personal path may not
be a simple either/or decision. In Dr Ghazi's case, he did not allow
himself to feel forced into choosing *either* his family business and
his merchant heritage *or* his personal passion for science. Instead,
he found, through years of reflection, study, experimentation and hard
work, a path that combined both into a single satisfying, rewarding
career.

In the end, Ghazi Binzagr discovered the leader within himself by
following those wondrous 'signs on the horizon' of which the Qu'ran
speaks. They led Ghazi Binzagr on a fascinating journey that, eventually, took him back home – to the work he was always meant to do.

In his personal quest for the right leadership role, Dr Ghazi had to
make sure that he was contributing within the boundaries of the
status quo while at the same time adding new value and breaking
new ground through the interests and studies that were close to his
heart. In this way, he kept his personal dream alive while serving the
here and now – balancing the past with the present and the future.

Through continual personal reflection, Dr Ghazi was able to capture
the best of both worlds. He kept his eyes open for the right circumstances that would enable him to connect his background with the
needs of his career and work. The lesson for other would-be leaders:
keep reflection central to your process of personal decision making,
keep your eyes open for the circumstances you seek and, when you
find them, take advantage of them.

The quest for true leadership

No two lifetime journeys are alike. Each path has its unique twists and turns, hurdles and challenges, highs and lows. But every inspiring leader is engaged in such a journey.

Waleed Bukhari, Asma Siddiki, Ghazi Binzagr – three very different personalities with very different interests, passions, skills and goals. Each has followed a unique career path, none of them predictable and obvious but all of them leading to destinations of surprising richness and satisfaction. And although none of the three is a public figure, all have played powerful leadership roles among the people and the organizations whose lives they touch – and each will leave the world a better place because of their presence and their work.

Where will *your* leadership journey take you? If you're like Waleed Bukhari, Asma Siddiki, Ghazi Binzagr or the other leaders whose stories I'll share with you, the chances are good that your final destination is a place you cannot now predict. But if you approach the journey in a spirit of openness, courage, diligence and passion, you're likely to find yourself, in the end, experiencing a life of adventure beyond what even your imagination can conceive.

2

What's your story? Beginning your journey of self-discovery

Whether consciously or not, anyone who aspires to leadership is engaged in a lifetime journey. It's a journey that begins with questions: What is your destination? Why are you heading there? What inspires you in life? What do you want to achieve? The sooner you begin to reflect on these questions and so make your journey a conscious and deliberate one, the better your chances of arriving at your destination with flying colours. Defining your personal aspirations long before you can attain them is not daydreaming – it's a crucial step toward creating a rewarding life. Make no mistake – true leaders are not born; they are developed, and as such they are self-developed.

Leadership often begins with an inspiring dream. And the most powerful dreams aren't about wealth. I've rarely seen people who aim purely at wealth end up happy. What intrigues and inspires us in the stories of people we admire is generally not the money they may have accumulated but rather the goals they attained, the obstacles they overcame and the legacies they left behind. These are what make a story worth repeating. The scars of battle are even more captivating and impressive than the medals of victory.

So if you aspire to leadership, I urge you not to make wealth your ultimate goal. Instead, strive to do work that is personally exciting and fascinating, and that helps to make the world a better place through the productivity and excellence of what you do. Aim for these things, and you will find that financial rewards tend to follow.

The story of my personal voyage offers a number of illustrative episodes and insights that you may be able to build on. Although I now help to run Banawi Industrial Group (B.I.G.), a family-held corporation in the manufacturing sector, I started my journey in the lowest levels of the organization – an important learning experience for me.

Learning from the lowest rung of the ladder

My work experience began when I was a high school student in Lebanon. I used to spend my summers back in Jeddah, working in various departments of our family business. I usually spent a good part of the day on the factory floor, getting my hands dirty, working behind specific machines and equipment, and developing practical knowledge of the products we made and the processes involved in manufacturing them to the highest possible standards.

This was an unusual experience, since the manufacturing sector barely existed in Saudi Arabia at the time. The dock workers charged with unloading our machinery when it came into port didn't even recognize what it was. Imagine being a high school kid working in a pioneering company in an industry that was largely unknown. It was a little bit peculiar, in that I couldn't compare notes about my summer jobs with my friends from school. At the same time, it was an exciting experience to watch the business growing alongside our nation – while I was growing up with both.

Later, I left the factory floor to work in other sections of the company, including accounting, sales and procurement. By the time I graduated from high school, I had a good sense of the push and pull of every function in our business. What makes a business go round? What kinds of practices lead to success? What kinds of mistakes matter most? I have seen it all from a grass-roots level – a valuable background that has served me well in my years as an executive.

One of the first lessons I learned was the value of personal relationships. The extent of camaraderie I experienced as a young beginner in the company was an eye-opener; my co-workers really took me on and taught me the different angles to the business. I soon realized that, if a leader can get the employees at every level of an organization to feel at ease with him or her, they will be far more happy, creative and productive.

Every business function had its own flavour. Accounting was valuable because it taught me how to translate our business efforts into financial results. I learned how to become comfortable with the numbers that measure business success, which is a crucial skill for any aspiring leader. The more you know about those numbers – and especially about what lies *behind* the numbers – the more effective you will be.

I particularly enjoyed working in manufacturing, because converting raw materials into a finished product is fascinating, an experience of transformation unlike anything most people normally witness in life. Although we as business leaders sometimes forget to give the people working behind the machines the credit they deserve, they have enormous skills and produce tremendous value from the enormous assets we entrust them with. That's why, every time I visit any of our operations, I'm always keen on shaking the hands of every employee behind a machine, just to ensure they understand that I truly appreciate what they do for our company.

The second function that really tickled my heart is sales. Investing in relationships pays a special dividend to any business, and particularly in the sales arena. When the customer likes you, you're in. To this day, I welcome the chance to be in front of customers – and the joy of helping to close a deal is always special!

Once when I was still in my teen years, during one of my summer jobs in sales, we were in competition with a non-local vendor for an important contract, and our sales team felt that it might give them an advantage if I joined them for the crucial meeting. Truly, our people did a great job presenting our company and products – so much so that I felt I had very little to add to what they had said. But I knew it was important for me to contribute something to the team effort, so before the meeting wrapped up I said to our potential clients:

> *As you can tell, I am way out of my league here. I'm pretty young and inexperienced, so you might not take me too seriously. But I will say one thing. I don't believe you'll find in our competitor the quality of the people that we have in our organization. If you entrust our company with this important work, I know that our team will work day and night to ensure your full satisfaction.*

The customer was impressed, and we clinched the deal.

Supplementing my classroom education with on-the-job learning made this period of my life extremely valuable for me. It left me with an attitude of curiosity and inquisitiveness that I retain to this day.

Those early years also shaped in a powerful way my attitude toward my career. They helped me understand that business is not a hobby

– it is serious work. They also led me to establish guidelines for achievement and challenging goals I had to strive to attain. I realized early that no one owes you anything – that you have to earn your stripes every day.

What makes you tick?

In my own journey of self-discovery, I've learned how important it is to discover what drives you internally – what makes you tick. When I speak to young people, I like to ask what subject at school really engages and excites them. Surprisingly, many have no clear answer. They haven't really got to know themselves, which makes me wonder how they will make wise career choices for themselves. Life is too precious to spend it doing work that does not make you feel alive every day.

This process of self-discovery begins with looking at and listening to yourself. It requires the ability and willingness to reflect on yourself and your life, a quality that is less common than it should be and that every would-be leader needs to begin practising at an early age. You'll need to think about what drives you: How would you define your dream job? What inspires you to reach high? What kinds of challenges engage you and bring out the best in you?

You'll also need to think seriously about your strengths and weaknesses, and about how you might balance conflicting career values: How important is money to you? How does it compare with such other job attractions as responsibility, advancement, independence and flexibility? Are you comfortable taking risks? Do you respond well to taking instructions? Do you prefer team projects or working alone?

Answering these questions honestly and objectively can be a challenge, but it's worth the effort to learn more about your greatest assets – your own mind and heart.

My journey started as a young college graduate when, due to unforeseen circumstances, I found myself in a position of some responsibility. I was appointed to a management post in our family company where I had worked a few summer jobs during my teen years. Soon I had to make decisions, to be accountable for the performance of others and to earn my stripes through results. Right from the start, I made a conscious decision to engage in our family company as any hired hand would. I wanted to earn my keep by performing well and climb the promotion ladder based on merit. I was surrounded by older colleagues who were answerable to me. Somehow I was careful not to take them for granted, and vice versa.

Over time, I began to take a closer look at my job in order to ensure that my decisions were carried out with sufficient authority. All through this period, I felt that I could make something better and bigger through what I was doing... and I often pondered!

Questions surfaced in my mind: 'How can I be better at what I'm doing?' and 'What kind of an example should I set for those working with me, so that they give their best?' This soul-searching was triggered by my eagerness to get more from the job and to give more to the job. This is how my journey was set in motion.

I then realized that I had a choice to make – either to keep doing what I was doing, discharging my responsibilities and exercising authority as best I could, or to develop my soft skills to levels that ultimately define the makings of leadership. It was a choice between accepting the status quo with some improvement, or evolving to be a true leader. I chose the latter. The first choice: the low road... the path most travelled... the cake walk. When we take this choice, we inevitably regress with time. The second choice: the high road... the path less travelled... the real challenge. When we take this choice, we evolve and soar. It is a personal choice that will shape our future and the future of those around us.

So the first leg in this boundless expedition compels you to be both self-critical and self-aware. What is self-awareness? In short, it is the training kit needed for embarking on this lifetime journey of self-development. By definition it is an ongoing experiment where we explore our individual personalities.

Because we are all different in the way we react to things, learn and assimilate information, it is imperative to spend time in self-reflection to gain a better insight into ourselves. Self-awareness is a prerequisite for effective communication, interpersonal relations and developing empathy for others. It is the DNA of all true leaders!

By the time you've developed a sense as to what career path you find attractive, test yourself in the real world. Pay close attention to the feedback you receive from others. This will help you discover how your talents may link up with realistic career options and where you are most likely to be able to add value to the world. Then, having chosen a path that expresses your aspirations in a realistic fashion, work hard to improve your skills through continual practice and learning.

This is the start of the journey of self-discovery that every aspiring leader must take – as you set sail on the long journey ahead. But there's much more to learn if you want to make your voyage a successful one.

Discovering your true interests and strengths isn't always easy. For many people, it is a matter of trial and error, with false starts and missteps along the way. Of course, those false starts are not necessarily wasted. In fact, they can often provide knowledge and experience that prove critical to your later success.

NABIL ALYOUSUF
Keep listening to your pulse!

In November 2007, HH Sheikh Mohammed bin Rashid Al
Maktoum, ruler of Dubai, convened a regional conference on
strategic philanthropy to which I was invited. The conference
itself was interesting, but one of the most valuable outcomes
for me was the opportunity to get to know Nabil Alyousuf,
a young member of Sheikh Mohammed's executive office
team who was helping to oversee the conference. Over time,
Nabil and I have built a lasting friendship, and I have
learned a lot from watching him work successfully across
various fields in both the private and public sectors.

Nabil Alyousuf is a good example of the fact that discovering what
makes you tick often takes time and experience – and that life may
involve unexpected twists that take you in directions you couldn't
anticipate. Here is how Nabil describes launching his career:

> *Twenty-five years ago when I graduated from high school,
> we depended on what friends and family recommended
> when it came to choosing our paths in life. Most of my
> brothers were engineers, and I'm good at science and
> mathematics, so I chose industrial engineering, a mix
> between business and engineering. However, I didn't
> end up practising engineering at all. When I came back
> from the United States after completing my education,
> I was employed by the Dubai Islamic Bank evaluating
> investment opportunities for the bank in the area of
> manufacturing. So my engineering knowledge ended up
> being useful background information for a career that was
> really centred on investments and finance.*

Many people have experiences like Nabil's. They discover, having studied one field, launched their careers in a second field, and then, perhaps, flourished in a third field, that all their areas of knowledge and expertise end up being relevant and helpful in the work they ultimately find most meaningful. So in your voyage of self-discovery don't dismiss any opportunity to learn as 'irrelevant' or 'useless'. The truth is that you can never know for sure what kind of knowledge may prove to be valuable at a later stage in your career – a stage that may be impossible to foresee.

At the Dubai Islamic Bank, Nabil began to discover some of the career lessons that have served him well in later years. For example, it can be a challenge to develop a sound confidence in your own judgement. Young people are often so lacking in self-confidence that they accept the judgements of others even when they go against their own deepest instinct.

Nabil Alyousuf recounts how he fell into this trap during his first leadership job, when he was asked to serve as CEO of a textile mill that the Dubai Islamic Bank had invested in:

> *I was young, and the general manager that I hired was a South African in his 50s, a production expert with a great deal of leadership experience and industry knowledge. So when he made some decisions that seemed incorrect to me, I doubted myself. For example, one of the things this manager decided to do was to lower the production rate to improve the percentage of fabric that passed a certain quality threshold. The idea was that a slower production process should enable a higher overall product quality.*
>
> *In truth, I didn't care for this decision. To my mind, production volume and quality should not be an either/or choice. You should be able to achieve both. But I deferred to the general manager because of his seniority. However, when we lowered the production volume, we produced less*

product, generated lower revenue and ended up suffering financial losses. The supposedly higher quality didn't make up for any of this.

That's when I decided to go ahead and do what made sense to me – to ask the workers for both a relatively high production volume and a high level of product quality. And it worked, despite what the general manager had said. It was the first of several disagreements he and I had, which ultimately led to my having to dismiss him. It was the first time I had to fire someone – an extremely hard task to learn to do.

But the larger lesson I learned from this incident was that sometimes you need to question and challenge the people around you – even your senior people – and trust in your own instincts.

This story from Nabil's early career reveals a number of significant lessons. For me, it reflects the fact that, in today's rapidly evolving business world, age and seniority are no longer decisive factors in separating leaders from followers. Prior to the 1990s, few young people had a shot at occupying the corner office reserved for the CEO or other high-level officials. Today, there are giant corporations in Silicon Valley run by executives in their 20s. As a result, younger managers are no longer expected to defer unquestioningly to the wisdom of their elders.

If you find yourself in the same position as young Nabil, don't examine the issues from a position of self-doubt or hesitation. Instead, start by asking the crucial questions and seeking objective answers: 'What is the right management approach to this situation? How will the proposed strategy work? What factual evidence supports this strategy as opposed to an alternative? What risks are involved?' Probing questions like these remove the issues from the personal or emotional level and make it easier for decision makers to focus cooperatively on the nuts and bolts of the problem.

How do you develop the ability to judge when it's time to follow your own instinct and when it's time to defer to the wisdom of others? It takes time, experience, reflection and, in most cases, a mistake or two – like the one Nabil Alyousuf made. Over time, you'll discover the kinds of situations in which your instincts are generally correct, as well as the areas of weakness in which you'll do best to be guided by others. Learning to evaluate yourself honestly and objectively will make this distinction easier to recognize and follow.

Nabil Alyousuf's next career stage involved a shift from the world of banking into the government sector. For eight years, Nabil worked for the executive office of HH Sheikh Mohammed bin Rashid Al Maktoum, ruler of Dubai and today vice-president of the United Arab Emirates. He eventually became the director-general of the office, a post he held for two years. This gave Nabil an exciting opportunity to develop his leadership skills in the service of a grand vision. Beginning in 2006, Nabil and the other members of the executive office team were asked to help Sheikh Mohammed develop and then realize a vision for the economic future of Dubai, under the general rubric of Dubai Strategy 2015. Sheikh Mohammed's mandate to the executive office was: 'Your job is to keep Dubai 10 years ahead of everybody else.'

This was, to say the least, an ambitious goal that demanded enormous creativity, intelligence, energy and vision. As Nabil explains, 'We needed to think about Dubai from every aspect – from a government and governance point of view, as well as from infrastructure and business environment to economic development.'

Nabil also recalls that the chairman of the executive office told him, 'Nabil, feel free to dream – and feel free to make your dream a reality.'

'That was a big motivation for me', Nabil says. In effect, Nabil was given the freedom to develop a wide-ranging vision and then to pursue it with the full support of the government of Dubai. It was the kind of assignment every aspiring leader dreams of.

Sheikh Mohammed also made the unconventional decision to select a team made up mostly of young people in their 20s and 30s to realize this vision, rather than relying on older leaders who had more experience but might also be more comfortable with traditional ways of thinking and acting. (Nabil himself was just 37 at the time.) The goal of the vision was bold, and so the spirit of the people developing it needed to be equally bold.

The work entrusted to Nabil and his young colleagues included the development and incubation of specific new initiatives and projects that could help Dubai realize the Sheikh's vision of an economically vibrant and progressive economic hub for the entire region – in particular, projects that created opportunities for the private sector. Nabil and the other members of the executive office responded with a series of imaginative programmes. For example, they developed the Dubai International Financial Centre (DIFC) to serve as a free zone that provides world-class financial services to individuals and companies from what the office calls the Dubai region, which includes countries within four hours' flight time from the Gulf – a vast region with a large and growing population and a significant accumulation of wealth, but lacking a proper financial centre with an effective set of regulations and a strong legal system. Similar initiatives were developed in other areas, including media and health care.

The global economic recession of 2008–09 has slowed the fulfilment of the vision that Sheikh Mohammed articulated and that Nabil and his colleagues worked to realize; it will take longer to achieve than originally planned. But progress continues to be made, and as a result one of the world's great business centres is being gradually transformed, creating business opportunities, jobs and new wealth for an entire region.

In 2009, Nabil returned to the private sector. Today he is chairman of Al Jal Capital, a private equity firm based in Dubai that specializes in identifying and developing investment opportunities in the Middle East, particularly in the health care, technology and education sectors.

As you can imagine, Nabil's broad range of experiences – from his training in engineering technology and working as a young banker at the Dubai Islamic Bank to serving as a visionary thinker and strategic planner for the government of Dubai – has helped prepare him well for the challenging task of building new industries that will help shape the economic future of the region.

Through each stage of his varied career, Nabil kept listening to what made him tick while diligently making the most of the opportunities presented to him. The combination of these two forces has produced a lifelong adventure that has been creative, productive and consistently engaging. The lesson for other would-be leaders: Work hard, respond to the call to leadership, and keep listening to the pulse of what makes you tick. You may not be able to predict where it will take you – but the journey is sure to be interesting!

Listen carefully to feedback of all colours

The process of self-development through the shaping, forming and honing of your personality can only be complete with the help of feedback from others. It requires openness to debate, criticism and advice. There is value in being constantly challenged, as long as you remember that such challenges are not about ego, personal status or self-affirmation, but about the quest for deeper understanding. If you're not willing to accept honest feedback, it's like choosing to listen only to your own voice speaking from the mirror. The words you hear may be soothing, but you won't learn very much!

Most people have a natural impulse to react poorly to criticism. It's easy to become defensive and hostile or to make excuses. I've worked hard to overcome this tendency in myself. Rather than reacting swiftly to negative feedback, I've learned to pause, take a moment for reflection and then ask a few probing questions like, 'What made you conclude that? Was there something specific I said which prompted your reaction? Do you have a suggestion as what I need to do differently?'

I may or may not agree with the answers to those questions – but I learn more by asking them than I would by moving into denial mode instead. Through practice, I've developed the ability not to respond negatively – even when people may be projecting their own negativity in my direction.

Train yourself to pay close attention to the feedback you receive from other people. Invite it rather than reject it. Many times it can be very educational, revealing truths about yourself that are almost impossible to perceive directly. You may discover that something you thought was a special strength of yours is really a weakness you need to work on. Or you may learn just the opposite, coming to recognize a strength you were unaware you had. (For some people, accepting the good news about their latent abilities can be just as difficult as absorbing criticism.)

Eventually, you will develop a pleasure in receiving honest, constructive feedback about your strengths and weaknesses. To someone who is eager to learn, such feedback is like a glass of water on a scorching summer day – a source of energy and refreshment.

Invest in yourself through lifetime learning

In your lifetime journey, traditional learning is very important. If you aim to be a leader, don't wait for others to invest in you – instead, invest in yourself by spending time, energy and money on training and education, whether technical, scientific, linguistic, managerial or financial. If you invest in yourself, then everything else you do will have added value.

In today's highly competitive, technologically complex, global world, higher education is essential for almost everyone. But choosing the right institution and the right curriculum can be a challenge. Many people assume that the most famous or prestigious place you can gain admittance to is automatically the best choice. For some students, it may be. You can obtain a fine education at a world-renowned institution like Harvard, Oxford or the Sorbonne – and the sterling reputation of such universities certainly adds lustre to your CV.

But for many, many people, a less well-known institution may actually be a better choice. My own alma maters – Rollins College in Florida, and Franklin College in Lugano, Switzerland – are not among the most famous colleges in the world. But I wouldn't trade the excellent education I received at those places for any other alternative – nor would I want to pass up the lifelong friendships I made during my years there.

When making their educational choices, many students don't devote enough time and energy to reflection. Ask yourself: 'What do I want to study? What kind of learning environment is best for me? What setting will bring out the best in me? What institutions are strongest in teaching my favourite subjects? Where are the most effective teachers in my field?' Delve as deeply as possible into these questions, seeking information and advice from as many reliable sources as possible. You may discover that your options for a fine education are far more numerous than you think.

Here is another example of the potential benefit of choosing a less-beaten path when it comes to education. After earning his master's degree at Thunderbird University in the United States, my friend Ghazi Binzagr (whose story I shared with you in an earlier chapter) decided to pursue a PhD in organizational dynamics. The question was: which graduate school should he attend? Ghazi received good advice from a professor at Thunderbird named William Voris: 'You know, Ghazi, you are like a rising star. You could go apply to one of the established universities right now, but they're established stars.

Established stars look for established stars. Rising stars should look for rising-star institutions. You gamble on each other.'

As a result, Ghazi attended a relatively new programme at the little-known New Mexico State University, headed by Mike Manning, a young professor who was trying to build a name for himself. Manning became Ghazi's mentor and allowed him to do things that would probably have been impossible at a more recognized university: Ghazi worked on projects directly with Professor Manning, co-taught with him at the master's level, and even redesigned and taught his own PhD-level class.

The lesson is clear: when making a choice about your education, don't automatically pursue the 'obvious' option. Learn as much as you can about the various alternatives, seek advice from a wide range of people you respect and, in the end, make the choice that is best for you rather than being swayed by the crowd.

Of course, traditional education is not the only source of learning. A diploma or even a college degree shouldn't be the end of your education but rather the beginning. In our ever-changing world, there is always something new and valuable to learn. Be constantly in an inquisitive state of mind. If you approach life and work in this spirit, every experience will be of value, helping you to build (rather than shed) your personal capital. Continually developing your skills is very important. As I like to remind the people I work with, 'Good luck is simply when preparation meets opportunity.'

In addition to improving your work-related skills, developing your personal qualities is just as important. Leadership is also about self-discipline, humility, courage and caring. Immerse yourself in problem solving early in your career – this is the training ground for opportunities later on. Those who shy away from tackling problems in their youth may never learn to recognize the opportunities hidden inside problems; instead, when troubles arise, they become subject to frustration and despair. Don't let this happen to you. When business challenges threaten to overwhelm you, remember: if you can manage the emotions, you can manage the issues.

We are all students of life, and we hope we never graduate!

The sweet taste of failure

People are often startled when they hear me refer to 'the sweet taste of failure'. It's a paradoxical phrase that requires a bit of explanation.

No one likes failure, of course. Whether big or small, any failure exacts a price. A career failure means a setback on the journey toward leadership. A business failure means a loss of profit, wasted time, damage to one's reputation, and missed opportunities. And when failures are not faced honestly and directly, and addressed promptly, they can have a cumulative impact. The discouraging impact of failure can lead to self-pity, a blaming mindset, and inertia, either in an individual or in an organization, and an uncorrected failure can cause the same mistake to recur, often leading to ultimate catastrophe.

So no one likes failure – and no one needs to be reminded to avoid it. But we *do* need to be reminded to take advantage of failures when they occur – which they inevitably do. And that's where 'the sweet taste of failure' comes in.

For me, the three best things about failure are *admitting it, learning from it* and *finding opportunity in it*.

Admitting it is the first crucial step. Once you accept the fact that you've made a mistake, you can stop being defensive, denying reality and wearing blinkers. Admitting failure is about being humble, human and authentic.

Have you ever known someone who *never* admitted failure? People like that are generally very difficult to get along with – proud, arrogant and sometimes harsh toward others. By contrast, people who are comfortable admitting their own fallibility are those we can respect and enjoy being around. By confessing their own humanity, they give you permission to be human as well – and that makes a genuine relationship possible. Showing vulnerability in this way does not take away from your personal capital – it builds it by increasing your credibility and the trust it earns. Think of this for a moment: people will eventually start saying, 'Someone who is honest with him- or herself will be honest with me.'

So don't be afraid to admit your failures. This is especially true within an organization. It can be tempting to try to cover up an embarrassing mistake in the hope that no one will ever find it out. Believe me, they will! And when they do your lapse in honesty will harm your reputation far more than the original failure could.

I make a point of telling everyone who works with me, 'Let's hear the bad news first. Good news can wait.' It's a philosophy every organization can benefit from – because once you've admitted your mistake you can learn from it. Or, as I also like to say, 'First accept the wrong. Then right the wrong.'

Many people and organizations don't do this. Because failure is so painful, they prefer to bury or ignore their mistakes. Don't fall into that trap! When your car is stuck in the mud, don't just keep revving the wheels, churning the muck and hoping that the next effort will free you. Instead, get out of the vehicle, take a few steps back and study the situation. Take time to examine what went wrong and figure out why it happened. You may need to change a habit, a way of thinking or a decision-making process that you take for granted. Confronting your failure is the best way to discover ways of growing and improving.

Finally, the smartest leaders learn how to find opportunities in failure. Wherever there is a problem, there is an opportunity lurking right behind it. That applies to many organizational failures. They represent weaknesses in our systems, our processes and our ways of doing business that offer opportunities for reinvention. If you really study the underlying causes of your failures, you may be surprised to discover that many of them point directly toward opportunities to create bold new successes in the future.

A diploma from the school of hard knocks

It might be nice if we could develop the qualities needed to be successful without ever experiencing failure, but life does not work that way! As I've personally discovered, the challenges never end – and that means the opportunities for learning and growth never end, either.

Back in 1980, I returned to Saudi Arabia with a newly minted MBA from the USA. And though I was very young, my father wasn't feeling well, so I was thrown into the driver's seat in a leading role in our family business early on.

The managerial, leadership and psychological challenges in family business are enormous, as most people realize. Combine the stresses of business in a competitive landscape with the stresses of family life, and you have a situation many people find emotionally fraught. In retrospect, I think some of the early decisions I made about how to handle this challenge were good ones.

First of all, after completing my MBA, I joined the company as a full-time employee on much the same basis as any hired hand. I simply asked, 'What does the market pay for a candidate like me – a person with an MBA, some US work experience under my belt, and some prior knowledge and experience of the company?' We drew up a compensation package, an incentive system and a series of clearly defined measures of performance based on those credentials, and we stuck to them.

It was important that I avoided joining the company with an attitude of 'The family, the founder and the organization owe me X, Y and Z'. I felt then, and still feel today, that nobody owed me anything – except the opportunity to prove what I could do and the value I could contribute.

Of course, managing the relationship between a father and son who are working together in a business is always complicated. As with any family connection, it goes through ups and downs. The trick is to prevent these from affecting the organization and the many other people, family members and non-members alike, who are depending on the company's success for their future welfare.

Looking back at the day-to-day relationship between the two of us – company founder and younger leader, father and son – I must say that my father, God bless him, gave me a lot of space. We were lucky enough to work together for about 10 years before my father decided to retire from his executive duties, and we managed to maintain our mutual respect and a feeling of deeply shared commitment to one another and to the corporation through all those challenges. There were certainly times when we had to take a step back, draw a deep breath and refuse to allow the heat of the moment or the emotions of disagreement to make us say something we'd regret. Later, when we would re-engage in a cooler mood, we always found a solution that we could both live with and that would benefit the company in the long run.

As I've already said, if you can manage the emotions, you can probably find a way to manage the issues. But if you focus on only managing the issues without managing the emotions, you tend to be distracted by the emotions you are trying to ignore, which can cloud your judgement and lead to needless mistakes.

Of course, it took me time to develop this degree of wisdom and understanding. In the beginning, I had no clue how to deal with my emotions in a business setting. It's not that I was excessively emotional or prone to flying off the handle; I was always a somewhat self-controlled person. But when I started to experience success early on, it got the better of me. I began to develop a bit of an attitude of 'I know what I'm doing. I don't need to listen to other people.' I fell into one of the most common traps that talented people in business (and other fields) fall into – the trap of hubris.

Luckily, I didn't go too far down that path. Two kinds of clues helped snap me back to self-awareness.

One came from the people around me. I began noticing that people were starting to read me wrong – responding negatively to things I said or did, or reading my intentions quite differently from how I understood them. For example, when I used business terms and language I'd learned during my MBA studies in meetings and presentations around the office, I noticed a barrier rising up between me and my colleagues. Some simply didn't understand the terminology I was throwing around; others thought I was behaving a bit like a young know-it-all; and still others resented the idea that I might be trying to 'Westernize' our company or transform it into something quite different from the founder's vision. None of these were my intention, but that's how I came across to some people.

When I found that I wasn't getting the kind of responses from people that I expected, I said to myself, 'I must be coming across in a way that is sending false signals. This is not me.' And I realized I had to change the ways I was communicating with people.

The second clue arose when business problems proved to be more complicated and more difficult to solve than I expected. When you become overconfident, you start assuming too much, and when you assume too much you start saying, 'Well, this project is really simple', which is usually not the case. The result is that you become a bit sloppy with some of the execution details and, the next thing you know, an initiative that should have been a success is struggling for survival. When this begins to happen more than once, it's a likely sign that you've allowed yourself to be infected with hubris.

Fortunately, I had a fair amount of self-awareness – a bit more, perhaps, than the average person of my age, and when these clues began to mount up I paid attention to them and responded. At some point, I just said, 'You know what? I'm going to start to be self-critical. I'm going to start to examine what I do at every meeting and every session, looking for the mistakes I've made and the opportunities I've missed.'

Once you take this all-important step, you start to become good at self-assessment. That's how the real journey starts.

Develop the habit of assessing yourself at key milestones and after important meetings, decisions, encounters and challenges. Be your own most rigorous judge, and no one else's harsh judgement will ever bother you again.

I was further reminded of the importance of perpetual learning and self-assessment when I made a serious misstep in the middle of my own career – a misstep from which, fortunately, I've been able to recover.

In the mid-1990s, I decided it was a good time for me to take a step back from the day-to-day management of B.I.G. I didn't do it to relax. Actually, it was a time when I had become very interested in scholarly pursuits, especially related to Islamic philosophy and culture. This was the time when I began to understand the true value of reflection and the larger perspective that gives meaning to every-thing we do. Scholars of the past offered enormous insights into these issues and how they affect human character and its strengths and weaknesses. Thrilled by these discoveries, I wanted to devote more time to reading, study and research, and over a period of three years I accumulated a lot of knowledge that has since helped me to be a better person as a husband, parent, friend and colleague. I felt I could create a business environment at B.I.G. in which others could assume most of the hands-on management responsibilities I had been handling, allowing me to focus on long-term strategy. The board supported my plan. But looking back, I see that I didn't handle the transition away from day-to-day management duties very well.

In particular, I didn't properly assess the company's readiness for the new leadership role I had envisioned, and I underestimated the extent to which my fellow workers banked on me as a leader and a mentor. I assumed too much – one of the most common mistakes that leaders make, but one that can cause serious problems in an organization.

As a result, our corporate culture, which I'd invested years to build and which had made our company successful, was compromised. Without allowing enough time for people to adjust to the changes, I put a layer of management between myself and many of the people I had nurtured over the years. The changes alienated my colleagues, led excellent people who'd started their careers with me to depart, and caused company performance to suffer.

In time, the combination of pressure from the company board and my inner sense of remorse over my responsibility for the problems caused me to return to a more involved leadership role at B.I.G. The corporate restructuring that I subsequently led has been a tremendous learning experience for me. With the help of God and the support of the good colleagues around me, we managed to turn around the company within a year.

This was a case in which we transformed a problem into an opportunity. So, really, there is such a thing as 'the sweet taste of failure' – and I can vouch for it! Of course, it would have been better if I hadn't made the mistake from which we had to recover in the first place. But confronting failure and using it as an occasion for growth is the next best thing.

Among other important lessons I learned from this experience is the reminder that reflection leads to better resolution. In retrospect, I realize that I made my decision to step away from my day-to-day management role too quickly and without adequate reflection. I hope this book will encourage readers to devote more time to self-examination and thoughtful analysis of the challenges or the choices they face, rather than rushing too hastily into decisions that may affect their lives and the lives of many other people for years to come.

The true meaning of 'career'

If you practise the principles described in this chapter, you'll come to understand the deeper meaning of the word 'career'. It's not about merely finding a job, getting paid a lot or having easy and pleasant work to do. It's about discovering the leader in you – figuring out what your true talents are and forging a path, through peaks and troughs of accomplishment, that will enable you to take the fullest advantage of those talents. In this way, you will create a career that brings the greatest benefits both to you and to the world around you. And this is the most reliable source of satisfaction in life, since self-esteem is *always* a by-product of personal achievement.

If a career is a lifetime journey of self-discovery, then a great career is like an expedition to Everest – an epic journey of many miles, facing unknown difficulties, that requires profound courage and deep strength of commitment. Experience and history show us that the human mind has the capacity to undertake and successfully complete such a journey. But the first few miles are the hardest! If you struggle during the early days of your lifetime journey, don't give up. Career changes may be unavoidable and beneficial – though don't make too many, or you may find yourself having to travel the first few miles over and over again. Once you are on the right path, remember to think about the amazing view you will enjoy from the summit of one of the world's greatest mountains. Let that vision inspire you to keep going – one step, one mile, one day at a time.

If you had the chance to write your own biography, what kind of story would you want it to tell? This is your chance to answer that question – and to make the dream into a reality. So start now!

3

The art of reflection, and other keys for the journey

Career stories like those I've shared in the last few pages illustrate another important principle: when facing a significant decision, take the time to reflect. You'll be glad you did.

In today's fast-paced world – in an age of multi-tasking, digital communication and instant gratification – many people seem to have lost sight of the importance of reflection. I think some people aren't quite sure how to go about it. Reflection seems to go against the tide of today's world, yet it is an essential skill for managing your own career wisely, as well as for serving as an effective leader to others.

Let me share a little of what I've learned from a lifelong effort to practise reflection and enjoy the benefits it offers.

Reflection is fundamentally a journey within. Like the lifetime journey we've been describing, it starts with the process of self-assessment and the questions it raises: What choices must I make in life? What inspires me? What skills come most naturally to me? What are my most serious weaknesses? Which qualities in myself am I most proud of? What do I hope to achieve in my career?

When you are young, your life is probably filled with activities, many of them important, others mere distractions – school, sports, family events, social gatherings, outings with friends, music, entertainment, work and travel. It's easy to fill your days and evenings with such busyness and then sink into oblivion the moment your head hits the pillow. However, a life without time for reflection is a mistake – like a frame without a picture. It leaves you vulnerable to drifting without aim, following the crowd and taking the path of least resistance rather than charting your own purposeful course through life.

So from an early age begin to develop the habit of reflection – of taking time to turn away from the world and its many enticements, and instead journeying within yourself in search of the core of meaning that defines you.

One way of practising this habit is through a daily mini-reflection. This simply means setting aside a few minutes every night to reflect on your day. Review your activities, and ask yourself: What did I accomplish? What did I learn? Did I do anything good for another person? Or did I, deliberately or inadvertently, cause pain or hardship to another? Do I have any misgivings about my behaviour? Did the way I spent my day strengthen my mind, personality, character and body, or erode and weaken them? Did I carry out any plans I made for the day, or did I allow myself to be distracted by outside influences? Did I manage circumstances, or did I let circumstances manage me? Do I go to sleep tonight feeling closer to my goals in life – or was today a day of wasted opportunities and drift?

If you practise this kind of mini-reflection, there will be times when you are pleasantly gratified by the thoughts and feelings that crowd your mind at day's end. You'll sleep well and arise refreshed. In other cases, you may find yourself dissatisfied or even embarrassed by the way you spent your day. Your sleep may be somewhat restless

– but you will probably wake up in the morning with a stronger resolve to make the next day a more productive, positive one. Over time, concluding each day with a mini-reflection will make you a stronger, happier and more fulfilled person.

Such mini-reflections on the value of a single day may seem trivial at first glance, but a lifetime is made up of nothing but individual days. Their cumulative value ultimately determines the value of an entire life. This simple but essential reality underlies the corporate mission statement we have adopted at B.I.G.: 'To Add Value in Everything We Do Every Day'. As a company, we recognize that, if we can do this consistently, then over time we hope to build a great organization. In the same way, if you can add value to everything you do every day, then over time you will write a memorable and fulfilling personal story of achievement, satisfaction and perhaps even greatness.

However, even more important than daily mini-reflections are the major times of reflection we need to practise whenever we face an important decision affecting our lives or our work. One example from my own journey occurred at a crossroads moment in life – after I graduated from college.

I was 22 years old and had graduated from Rollins University in Florida with a bachelor's degree in a dual major – business and political science. I had supplemented my classroom learning with summers spent working at B.I.G., learning a lot about myself and about the kinds of businesses the company was engaged in. I felt well prepared by my academic studies. But the question was: what to do next? It's the same challenge faced by millions of new young graduates every year.

By this time in my life, it was clear to me that I wanted to pursue a career in business, but the nature of the next step on my career ladder was far from clear. Should I go right to work at B.I.G., or should I instead pursue additional education, such as by enrolling in a master's degree programme with the goal of earning an MBA degree?

Taking a job at B.I.G. was the choice my father recommended to me. There would certainly be an interesting and challenging assignment available for me if I were to select this route. Having worked at B.I.G. before, I was well known to the people there, and I was familiar with many of them. And of course, I would have the option of returning to the classroom at a later date if I felt it was necessary. Why not take the initiative and get a few years of full-time work experience under my belt?

Nevertheless I had other concerns that led me to draw back from this decision. In thinking about my future at B.I.G., I was very aware of how my personal qualities and circumstances might affect my career. I was still quite young and lacked the breadth and depth of experience that most other business managers bring to the table. As a member of the founding family of the company, I would be under special scrutiny from my colleagues, who might wonder if I had the same degree of talent, judgement and wisdom that my father had exhibited in building the business. Older colleagues might be inclined to test my mettle. And I knew there were some specific areas of business knowledge that I needed to improve, including financial management and organizational development. If I immediately accepted a manager's job at B.I.G., I might be out of my depth.

Thankfully, I sensed that this was an important decision. I didn't rush into making a choice. I took time to reflect, thinking deeply not just about my personal feelings but also about the situation as a whole. Among other factors, I weighed the reality that my father was getting older and was beginning to show signs of diminished health, which made him especially eager to bring his eldest son – a potential successor – into the company as soon as possible. And I also researched the realities and the options surrounding graduate study in business, exploring all the possible permutations of an educational programme that might meet my needs.

Over time, an option I hadn't been aware of came to my attention – an accelerated MBA programme that included intensive study during two summer semesters. This choice offered the best of both worlds: an opportunity to improve the depth of my business knowledge combined with a minimal delay on my path from school to the world of full-time work.

With my father's consent, I enrolled in this programme. I earned my MBA and soon thereafter joined B.I.G., better equipped and more confident than I would have been had I gone straight from college into the workplace. It was a milestone decision for my early career that benefited enormously from taking the time to reflect.

For true reflection to occur, you need to disengage from the ordinary activities of life. Everyone will find his or her best way of doing this. For me, the surroundings of nature are most conducive to reflective thought. If I have the time and opportunity to travel up into the mountains and spend a day or two in solitude, any significant decision I have to make will benefit. I think many people find renewed strength, serenity and wisdom in contact with nature. And you don't have to be able to take a vacation in order to tap into the power of a natural environment. A pleasant stroll without the interruption of your mobile phone or a quiet afternoon sitting in a garden can be just as cultivating.

Reflection as I am describing it is not a form of meditation or prayer. Rather, it is simply a way of making space for your mind, so that better, more deeply considered decisions can emerge. Sometimes it's helpful to use pencil and paper to record your thoughts about whatever issue you are facing. (I suppose for some people a computer might serve equally well – but for true reflection be sure to set aside the e-mail, the internet, the Facebook and YouTube accounts, and the computer games!) Many people like to use the traditional approach, first popularized by one of the United States' founding statesmen, Benjamin Franklin, of listing the pros and cons of any alternative in two columns, as an aid to reflection and a way of making the key decision factors clear and concrete. Reflecting on the decision *slowly* rather than rushing to make a choice allows your creative juices to flow; new options and overlooked factors often bubble to the surface, and these can sometimes change your thinking dramatically for the better.

When is it important to reflect? Minor, routine decisions usually don't require reflection, but important decisions – those that will affect many people, that will shape your own future for years to come, that involve grey areas of subtle judgement not just stark black-and-white options, or that involve consequences that may be difficult or impossible to reverse – call for time out for reflection. As you make this style of decision making into a habit, you'll become better and better at recognizing when reflection is required.

Shortly after I was asked to take over the direction of B.I.G. (I was in my late 20s at the time), I faced a major set of decisions regarding the kinds of businesses we would or would not pursue. This was another moment in my career when reflection was essential – in this case, because of the relative complexity of the options and their significance for the future of B.I.G. and its people.

In particular, I found I had to decide whether to retain certain business operations that were parts of B.I.G. but didn't necessarily fit our strategic plans for the future. The right path was far from obvious. On the one hand, the two businesses most affected were profitable, or at least breaking even. (If they had been clear money-losers, it would have made my choice simple!) However, their profit margins fell short of the hurdle rates we'd established at the time for return on investment (ROI), an important financial benchmark, and even our best managers couldn't come up with a workable plan for dramatically improving those margins. We were competing against some strong rival companies, and couldn't see a way of developing unique skills or knowledge that would enable us to redefine our competitive advantage. It seemed we were stuck at the current plateau – not losing money, but not making much and not achieving notable progress, either.

The bulk of the evidence suggested to me that divesting these business areas would be the wisest decision, but that was a hard choice to make. B.I.G. had been operating these companies for years. The managers were our long-time colleagues. Our board members would feel that abandoning these businesses was almost like turning our back on friends in need.

Torn by these conflicting impulses, I took time away from the office to reflect on the issues and how they would affect the long-term future of B.I.G. and its people. The more I studied the facts, pondered alternative pathways and weighed the pros and cons, the more comfortable I felt with the need to act.

In the end, I developed a plan in collaboration with my colleagues that made the most sense for our company. We sold one of the two underperforming businesses to a corporation for which it was a more strategic fit. The other we kept (largely because of the valuable location of the operating plant), but restructured and reduced in scale. Of course, we worked closely with our human resources people to make sure that employees affected by the reorganization received help and support in making the transition to new jobs elsewhere.

Today, many years after we made this tough call, I think it's clear to everyone at B.I.G. that the future direction of the company was improved by letting go the two businesses that were distracting us from our core strategy. It was a good decision that would probably not have been possible without taking ample time for reflection.

Plenty of pressures in the business world will make it hard for you to practise reflection as much as you should. Colleagues will press you to make quick decisions when they are eager to move ahead on opportunities they perceive as urgent. Moves by competitors will sometimes drive you to react impulsively out of fear of being left behind. Resist these pressures. When confronted with a decision to be made, always ask, 'How long do I have to make this choice?' Get all the time you can, and use it wisely. Sometimes you'll find that, before the decision bell rings, circumstances change in such a way as to make the right choice much more obvious, even inevitable.

Decision making is one of the most important skills of a leader. You need the courage and self-confidence to make decisions in conditions of uncertainty or incomplete information – which are the kinds of conditions in which almost all important choices must be made. You also need the humility to reconsider decisions when necessary and to change them when possible. Yet at the same time you don't want to change decisions so often that people begin to perceive you as someone who simply agrees with the last person you speak with.

Taking the time to reflect thoughtfully before making any major decision helps avoid the need to make U-turns later, and it wins you permission from colleagues and partners to change your mind on the relatively rare occasions when it is unavoidable.

Reflection produces many other benefits. It helps you understand both the world and yourself much better, enabling you to feel more at ease with yourself and better able to achieve the level of authenticity that is one of the distinguishing marks of a leader. This, in turn, helps you maintain a sense of humour, of balance and of perspective – crucial traits every leader must have.

Reflection also makes you better able to appraise honestly and objectively the strengths and weaknesses of the people you work with – as well as your own. A true leader must have a clear-eyed understanding of the value of each asset and resource at his disposal. That includes the people, their talents, organizations, systems, functions, processes, products and physical assets like factories, equipment, property and so on. No leader has infinite resources available, and business is about creating value – so business success must begin with an accurate assessment of existing values.

There's an old Arab saying: If you don't recognize the falcon, you may think it's a pigeon – and mistakenly grill it! Reflecting at moments of decision can help you avoid this kind of costly error.

DR EBTISAM DKAHKHNI
Combining the best of both worlds in healing minds

The story of Dr Ebtisam Dkahkhni illustrates, among other themes, the power of reflection in helping to empower the inner qualities of an Unknown Leader.

When I first got to know Ebtisam, she appeared to me to be a mature young woman. She was the closest friend of my cousin's sister. Three years younger, I liked to visit my cousin at his home in Jeddah during the summers. In our teenage years, age differences are multiplied in importance, so my cousin's sister and her friend Ebtisam looked down on us boys and treated us as annoyances to be brushed aside and sometimes laughed at.

Years passed. We all grew up, and I lost touch with Ebtisam. Eventually, I was asked to serve on a think tank headed by the then governor of the Mecca Region of Saudi Arabia. Our mandate was to give the governor balanced advice on problems and issues related to the private sector – in particular, the issue of how best to harness the talent and energy of young people in positive ways without wasting it.

Members of the committee began offering a variety of ideas on the topic. When the governor turned to me for an opinion, I said respectfully, 'I come from a school of thought that says, before a physician prescribes a treatment, he needs to know who the patient is and listen to his or her complaints. So why not invite young men and women from our region to attend a conference and tell us their concerns directly? Then we can also offer them reliable professional counsel and advice.'

The governor liked this idea and asked me to chair the project, so we developed a plan for a conference focused on young people between the ages of 18 and 26. A couple of my friends on the committee agreed to help fund the project, and we were soon up and running.

What followed was a remarkable team effort, facilitated by the support of the executive director of the think tank. I said, 'We need a scientific committee of people who know this field – sociologists, psychologists, educators, behavioural scientists and other experts to help us interpret what we hear and present a compelling theme and a complete programme in response. Let's enlist a group that is half men, half women, to ensure a balanced analysis.'

We started asking around and interviewing people, and someone suggested Dr Ebtisam Dkahkhni – my cousin's friend from way back. And what a surprise when I researched her credentials and discovered that she was indeed an immensely qualified expert on the challenges facing young people. We quickly enlisted her to support our effort.

Now the situation had changed – I was no longer a kid but a grown-up! As chair of the project, I worked Dr Ebtisam and all of our other fellow committee members very hard, asking them to contribute their very best insights and wisdom for the benefit of our young people. They responded enthusiastically, many of them saying, 'You demanded a lot from us – and we loved every minute of it!' That goes in particular for Dr Ebtisam, whose depth of knowledge and sensitive understanding enriched our work enormously.

Having reconnected after the long lapse in our friendship, we have stayed in touch with one another ever since. Dr Ebtisam was one of the first people who came to my mind when I began scanning my personal horizon to identify some of the Unknown Leaders I most greatly admire from many diverse fields.

When you ask Dr Ebtisam her thoughts about leadership, her first response is to say, with a modest smile, 'I never considered myself a leader', but the more you learn about her life and work, the more you recognize her leadership qualities, and the ways in which she has used these qualities as a pioneer in the field of psychology, especially among women in our part of the world.

Ebtisam grew up in Jeddah, Saudi Arabia, at a time and in a place when most people assumed that the role played by a woman would be fairly strictly limited. Her father, himself an educated man, believed in the value of education for females (up to a point), but also assumed that women's natural role was in the home rather than in the workplace.

Ebtisam's mother took a slightly different attitude. Although she did not know how to read or write, she wanted her daughters to enjoy the richest education they could possibly experience. At the end of every school year, when Ebtisam's father would say, 'Well, that's enough schooling for you girls', her mother would interject, 'No, no. You should keep going another year.' Dr Ebtisam recalls that encouragement as a vital factor in her own success, calling her mother 'the light bulb in my life'. 'She was a wise woman and wanted me to have what she did not have', Dr Ebtisam adds.

As for Ebtisam herself, she had always been gifted with the power of reflection. Deep self-analysis and thoughtful consideration of what inspired and motivated her had told her that she wanted a career, perhaps as a journalist or writer. Although the usual assumption of the time that early in life was the right time for a girl to marry – in fact, the earlier the better – Ebtisam delayed her marriage until after she'd completed her high school diploma, which was 'a bit late' by the standards of the time.

Ebtisam and her husband went to the United States to continue their schooling. Ebtisam went to the University of Houston for her bachelor's degree, initially planning to pursue the dream of writing, but a few courses in psychology led her to a period of new reflection that ultimately changed her thinking. 'I just fell in love with the field, and decided that I was going to become a psychologist.' She redirected her academic work in the United States toward this new goal. She earned a bachelor of science degree in psychology and then pursued a Master's degree in educational psychology, with a special focus on her primary interest, the nature of intelligence. After doing research with school children and adolescents, she realized that the emotional well-being of children profoundly influences their abilities and performance. She then moved to Los Angeles, California, where she pursued a second Master's degree and a PhD in clinical psychology, all while studying psychoanalysis in her free time and working two to three days a week. She followed this with a fellowship at the respected Menninger Clinic, then located in Topeka, Kansas.

In the midst of all this, her marriage fell apart. However, Ebtisam maintained her determination to learn and grow professionally even through the painful end of her marriage – the first divorce in her family.

It was a time of very hard work for Dr Ebtisam, juggling classroom studies, teaching, intensive research, clinical work with patients under the careful supervision of an amazing psychologist, and the responsibilities of being the single mother of a small child. But Dr Ebtisam loved it all. 'I was driven by a dream and a passion that I had to just go ahead and pursue', she says. 'This is what life is about. There are always challenges and difficulties, but I think what keeps one centred is passion and the determination it creates.' In addition, Dr Ebtisam credits the support she received from her family – her parents, her brother, and later her son.

Dr Ebtisam took full advantage of all the resources for personal growth and self-development she could find in the United States, pushing herself to learn all she could about mental processes, human behaviour and a wide range of mental conditions, from depression and psychosis to autism.

By 1998, Dr Ebtisam had finished her fellowship at Menninger, and in 1999 she returned to Saudi Arabia. She resumed life in Jeddah as a proud Saudi woman, but one whose knowledge and outlook had been broadened and deepened by a decade of intensive study, life experiences good and bad, and an immersion in a very different culture with many strengths and weaknesses of its own – as well as continual reflection on the meaning of these experiences in the larger narrative of her life.

When she sought to resume her career in Jeddah, she found that the professional status of psychologist was then almost non-existent in Saudi Arabia:

> *I realized there was just one non-Saudi male who had*
> *a PhD in psychology and another male who was just*
> *a couple of years ahead of me. Young women who had*
> *graduated with bachelor's degrees in psychology were*
> *working in the field. By contrast, in the United States,*
> *only psychologists with Master's degrees can work with*
> *patients. In Saudi Arabia, there was, until recently, no*
> *Master's degree offered in psychology.*

Ebtisam decided that psychological training in Saudi Arabia needed to grow. She set about doing it, one student at a time.

She became an adjunct assistant professor of psychology at Dar Al-Hekma College in Jeddah, a progressive institution for women with strong ties to a number of universities in the United States. 'I was attracted to Dar Al-Hekma', Dr Ebtisam says, 'because they've given women exposure to all kinds of educational opportunities, both during the regular school year and during summers when they can travel abroad to take courses at great universities like Harvard. They're really trying to teach those young women to be entrepreneurs, to be lawyers, to be leaders in every field.' Dr Ebtisam served on the faculty for six years, teaching students in the classroom and working with patients in the adjacent hospital.

Because the system of clinical training was different from the one she'd encountered in the United States, Dr Ebtisam found herself 'almost inventing' new ways of educating the young women she met. For example, she discovered there was a need for clinicians trained in assisting patients to handle standard psychological testing instruments accurately. She explains:

> *We have a lot of patients who cannot read and write well, so when we give them a paper-and-pencil test someone knowledgeable needs to sit with them to read it for them and make sure they understand what is being assessed. This applies to tests like the Minnesota Multiphasic Personality Inventory, the Myers–Briggs assessment, or any standard IQ test. So I invented a new job that I called psychological technician, and began training young women at the college to fill this role. In this way, they do not harm patients by their lack of experience and training. At the same time, they are learning more about psychological testing as well as providing a valuable service that our patients need. With my supervision, they carried out the testing, and then I would interpret the results and type the reports.*

Dr Ebtisam was pleased with the response:

> *I found a number of girls who were really passionate about what they're doing. One was in the hospital working as a psychologist when I started mentoring her, although she hadn't received the kind of training she really needed. She was eager to learn, so I was very honest with her. I told her, 'Look, a lot of what you're doing with patients is wrong.*

It's not your fault. You need more and better training. And I think you have a lot of potential, and I can see you have the passion and the desire to learn, so I'm going to mentor you. But in the meantime, I want you to stay within your knowledge base. Later, after I've taught you all I can, I will be happy to support you to go abroad or continue your studies wherever and however you want.' She was really open to that, and she reminded me of how passionate I was for education. Now she has 10 years of experience under her belt, and she is doing much better. I'm very proud of her.

At the same time that Dr Ebtisam was pioneering new ways of teaching young women, she was also working hard to build a base of private practice with patients of her own. This posed different challenges. She recalls:

When I first came back to Jeddah, people warned me that it would be very hard. They said all kinds of things that turned out not to be true. I was told I might open an office and go without patients for months, because people in Saudi Arabia just don't believe in seeking help for their psychological problems. And I was told that, if people do make an appointment, they'll think nothing of missing it without notice. After hearing warnings like this, I really expected the worst.

Dr Ebtisam listened to the warnings, but she believed deeply, based on personal experience and observation, in the healing value of professional psychotherapy, and she was convinced that people in every society can benefit from it. Upon reflection, she determined to create a system that would help Saudis realize and appreciate psychotherapy, even if it took time and lots of hard work to make it happen.

The results were surprisingly good. 'It's amazing how fast people can learn', Dr Ebtisam says. It all happened through her college and by word of mouth. Dr Ebtisam offered public lectures and symposiums for both the general public and professionals (psychologists and psychiatrists), and these attracted large audiences of curious men and women. Soon word travelled throughout the community about the useful services being offered by this well-spoken, highly educated Saudi professional. Within a relatively short time, Dr Ebtisam's appointment book began to fill up. Individual men and women came asking for advice and help with psychological problems of various kinds, parents brought their children for diagnosis and therapy, and couples started coming for help with marital difficulties.

As for keeping appointments, 'Nobody can come without an appointment', Dr Ebtisam says. 'And they come on time, which I was told nobody does. When people know that this is their time, and if they don't show up they miss the appointment until next week, then they learn to come!'

Dr Ebtisam continued her pioneering work as a teacher, trainer, mentor and therapist in Jeddah until 2011, when she moved to Riyadh after her mother passed away. Now she is reinventing her career yet again. She works at King Faisal Hospital, providing psychological services in several areas, including services for patients undergoing lung, liver and heart transplants as well as for oncology patients. She is also working with her colleagues to establish the first psychiatric diagnostic centre for children in the hospital, designed to provide assessments and psychological testing needed for the diagnosis and treatment of children. 'Without a centre like this', she says, 'so many children get misdiagnosed and lost in the shuffle.'

Having grown up in one culture, been trained and educated in another, and now practising her profession back in her native land, Dr Ebtisam has lived her whole life as a pioneer of sorts. Rather than fitting neatly into a prearranged niche, she has been challenged to discover her own place in society, taking the skills and knowledge she has developed over a lifetime and finding ways to put them to use in a new setting, for the benefit of a different population. It requires a degree of imagination, creativity and vision that you cannot learn from a university course but which you must develop from the inside out – and which Dr Ebtisam has to a high degree. It also requires the willingness to engage repeatedly in reflection, closely examining the meaning of each new change in circumstances and adjusting one's life journey in response.

'I don't consider myself a leader,' Dr Ebtisam says again, 'but as a teacher I've seen the dreams in the eyes of young women, and I like the opportunity to help them pursue those dreams.' She adds:

> *I also like the chance to bring the best of two cultures together. My life in the United States changed me in many ways and enriched me as a person and human being. Yet I think it's sad to see some elements of traditional Saudi culture, such as the family structures and the ways neighbors and communities relate to each other with care and compassion, becoming somewhat weaker and disintegrating. I'd like to take the best of the two worlds and combine them, embracing independence and freedom with responsibility, reaching out to others with compassion combined with caring about the community and keeping family connections and ties. I hope the younger generation will really remain rooted while taking advantage of the best things that the broader world has to offer. If there is any message in my life and work, perhaps this is it.*

The life and work of Dr Ebtisam offer some powerful lessons that are relevant to all of us. The more our society opens up as a result of globalization and the accelerating pace of modernization, the more we're bound to encounter lifestyles and values that differ from ours. We shouldn't let this risk cause us to stop engaging with the world, but we must engage responsibly, ensuring that our values serve as our anchor and our compass, helping us to remain safe and to head for true north even when the winds of change are battering us.

As Dr Ebtisam teaches us, the values of family life can be a great healer, enabling us to remain strong and intact as individuals and as a society, even in times of adversity. At such times, remembering to engage in reflection is the best way to ensure we keep a tight grip on those all-important values and on the power of our personal dreams rather than merely drifting with the tides of life.

Reflection, then, is one of the most important tools I've found for making any lifetime journey successful and rewarding. Here are some other keys for unlocking the doors on the path to leadership.

Find a mentor and you'll have a treasure trove for life

Find a mentor who can help you to evaluate yourself objectively. There is much to be learned from an older friend, colleague or associate who is willing and able to serve as a sounding board and counsellor. Many young people are shy about befriending members of the older generation. If you fall into this category, I urge you to overcome your hesitation. Don't just stand on the shore watching the waves come and go. Take the plunge! Seize the opportunities for cross-generational dialogue provided on college campuses and in the workplace. Young people can gain a great deal from insightful friendships with older people – and vice versa, I might add!

But choose your mentor wisely. The wrong adviser can hold you back rather than propel you forward – for example, friends who want you to mirror their own experience rather than grow beyond them, or those who are unfailingly sympathetic and therefore encourage you to remain in your comfort zone rather than taking on life's greatest challenges. Sympathy is nice – but a mentor should encourage you to engage with difficulties rather than shrink from them.

This explains the simple, memorable slogan that defines our mentoring philosophy at B.I.G.: 'Push and embrace.' Working with a mentor who gives you the benefit of 'tough love' by challenging your assumptions and pushing you to achieve the seemingly impossible can be painful – but it is also powerful. We'll talk more about mentoring as a tool for leadership development in Chapter 8. But let's remember, the saying 'No pain, no gain' goes beyond muscle toning into character building.

Weave your own network – the right way

Networking can be a powerful tool for self-development. It also allows you, when tackling a new challenge or opportunity, to expand beyond your own capacities. An aspiring leader needs to develop the most flexible and agile arsenal of tools and methods to draw upon in times of need. In today's complex global world, this is essential – and networking makes it possible.

However, networking is often misunderstood. Contrary to popular belief, networking is not about using other people but more about becoming boundary-less: as you take one day, you will have the chance to give back another. Networking is based on giving to others more than you take from them. The smart networker is interested in other people for their own sake and is happy when the opportunity arises to help them.

You probably know a few expert networkers. They are the people who will call you when they hear about a job you might be interested in, a contract your company might want to compete for, or an important piece of industry news that might affect your business. They are the ones who send you a newspaper or magazine clipping from a little-known publication because they think the contents might be useful to you. They are the ones who offer to help with a job reference, a phone number or e-mail address, or a 'good word' with a well-placed friend. In short, networkers are the people whose thoughtfulness, generosity and concern for others provide the social lubricant that helps make business friction-free – and successful.

In return, they enjoy the benefits that come to people who are widely and genuinely liked. Networkers are 'people people'. It's not a quality you can fake – but it is a habit you can develop in yourself through continual practice. Be an investor in good relationships. Your returns in the long run will far exceed many other investments out there.

In the end, networking is about relationships. It's about the con-nections among people that make things happen. These deserve to be taken seriously. Every relationship you enter is a choice that only you can make. It involves a commitment that will shape your mind, your personality and your future path in life – perhaps for good, perhaps for ill, perhaps in a small way, perhaps in a very significant way, but it will affect you in some way, which is why it deserves thoughtful consideration.

And note, too, that when you are young is when your choices about the relationships you enter will have the greatest impact on your life. This goes contrary to the way most people think. We feel that youth is a carefree time when decisions about friends and acquaint-ances can be made casually and with little thought – after all, there's so much time ahead in which to change our companions. But it's precisely because youth is a time of relative freedom that it's also a time when choices about relationships are most important. After all, when we are young, we have made relatively few commitments and we have enormous freedom to shape our future path in life – the work we will do, the values we will uphold, the goals we will pursue. But every relationship you enter begins to foreclose some of your future opportunities; each one can either expand or limit your future journey.

So if you are young, begin thinking now about the kinds of relationships you want to build your life around. There's no time like today to choose the path that leads toward the tomorrow of your dreams.

Develop a magnetic personal voice

Leadership is about people – about inspiring others to share your excitement about a powerful vision, and encouraging them to use their talents to help make that vision come true. Because the amount that any one person can do is limited, achieving great things requires the combined efforts of many people, driven by mutual goals and a clear understanding of the work to be done. And all of these challenges – inspiring others, encouraging them, sharing goals with them, and developing plans that are clear and understood by everybody – depend on communication, and especially oratory.

For this reason, the aspiring leader must begin practising communication skills at an early age. One recommendation is to learn from the masters. Study the speeches of history's most inspiring leaders. Notice how they used simple language, clear examples, heartfelt emotions and personal stories to connect with listeners. Read the persuasive appeals of great leaders from politics, business and other fields. Observe how they marshal the most effective arguments, knock down opposing arguments respectfully but firmly, and communicate to readers the bold vision that underlies their appeal.

You also need to seize opportunities to practise communication personally. Most people are terrified of public speaking. (In many surveys, 'giving a speech' is listed as the second worst nightmare – just a little behind 'death'!) Work to overcome this fear through familiarity. When you tackle a team project on your course, volunteer to be the one to stand before the class to present your findings and respond to questions. Participate in speaking contests and debates. Attend forums on social issues and practise expressing your own point of view.

If the school, college or university you attend offers special sessions to learn about and practise communication skills, take advantage of them. The Ambassadors Program at Effat University, which is supported by B.I.G. (and which I'll describe in more detail in Chapter 8), includes a special emphasis on helping students develop their communication skills, especially in the crucial area of spoken communication.

Over time, the fear of talking to a large group of people will gradually diminish. Take it from me, it never goes away completely, but that's all right. The edge of nervousness we all feel when everyone's eyes are upon us is natural and even helpful. It stimulates the flow of adrenalin that makes us energized, alert and excited. 'Butterflies in the stomach' help us do a better job of reaching the audience and are not to be feared.

Once you are in a leadership role, even a modest one, remember to *over-communicate* when you have an important message to share. Most people absorb only a fraction of the things they hear, see or read. Many times it is the third, seventh or tenth repetition of a message that finally touches the mind and heart of an individual. So, for example, if your organization is communicating a new vision, announcing a new policy, launching a new product, applying a new strategy or implementing a new quality programme, don't expect to explain it once and then stop. Instead, be prepared to describe the new initiative repeatedly, whenever you have the opportunity. These multiple explanations, in different contexts and using different examples, will help your team members gradually to grasp what the initiative means to them and how they are supposed to participate.

Eventually, you may get to the point when all, or nearly all, of the people around you have fully understood and accepted the message, but achieving this generally takes much more time and effort than we assume – as the most effective leaders among us know. If you hope to shape corporate culture, you need to be constantly communicating. Picture how a trickle of water, over time, carves the rock and creates a basin. Constant communication has the same deep and lasting impact.

Leaders also know the importance of speaking from both the head and the heart. Presenting the facts is necessary – but just as necessary are the feelings that give meaning to the facts. In the words of author Terry Pearce, 'While the mind looks for proof, the heart looks for engagement. While the mind looks for information, the heart looks for passion. While the mind looks for answers, the heart looks for experience. The mind makes a decision, and it's the heart that makes a commitment.'

So when you seek to persuade an audience to accept your position on an issue, to change their thinking or to follow your lead in a new direction, reach out with the heart as well as the head, showing how your message expresses values that you all share and promises mutual benefits that all will enjoy.

When B.I.G. first drew up plans for the transformation of the company with the goal of going public in the future, I invited all our managers to Bahrain to explain the process and win their support. There were several ways I could have approached the topic. I could have given a bunch of statistics about how going public affects the finances of companies. I could have listed the impressive names of other companies that have issued public stock. I could have quoted business professors or financial writers about the benefits of going public.

Instead, I chose a direct emotional appeal. I said:

> *You've got to understand why we're doing this. This is not just about preparing our company to go public one day. We're doing it so that, at the end of the day, each one of us can look back on our years at B.I.G. and say, 'I was so fortunate to be part of the story of an organization that started from modest beginnings and over five*

decades became a public company and a role model for other companies to follow – and one that gave me the opportunity to write my own story as part of that.' Having experienced a journey like this will be so gratifying – even more gratifying than achieving the ultimate goal.

When a message is graphed in vivid terms that anyone can identify with, it resonates.

One more point about communication. In today's digital age, many young people have come to rely on electronic tools for staying in touch with friends, family, classmates and colleagues. There's nothing wrong with these tools and the devices that enable them. Text messaging, e-mails and social media such as Facebook, Twitter and YouTube all have their place, and today's leaders are smart about using them often and effectively. However, too many young people seem to have lost sight of the power of face-to-face, human-to-human communication. I've seen co-workers sitting at desks just a few metres apart who prefer to send e-mails rather than speak directly, which makes no sense to me. When the message to be conveyed is extremely simple – 'Let's move tomorrow's meeting from 2 to 3 pm' – then a text message may be all right, but when anything more complex and significant is involved then a more direct, personal, engaged form of communication is essential. Better than e-mail is a phone call – and better than a phone call, whenever possible, is a personal conversation.

You'll find that you can learn much more about people – what motivates, interests, challenges, concerns and inspires them – when you spend time with them face to face. In a personal meeting, ideas and emotions have a way of flowing freely; problems rise to the surface, concerns get aired, alternative approaches get suggested, and underlying values get reaffirmed. By contrast, when you rely on text messages or e-mail, these kinds of nuances often get overlooked or buried. The result: minds and hearts fail to become engaged, and as a result projects often become delayed or derailed.

Think of friendships in business or in life as being like plants – they need water to grow, and the human form of water is time spent face to face, or at least voice to voice. In a world where there's never enough time, don't let digital activity drain time away from human contact.

Communication is continuous, whether we are aware of it or not. In fact, when you don't think you are communicating, you may be communicating the most powerful message of all. So being conscious of the messages you are sending at all time, and making sure that they are the messages you *want* to convey and that they are transmitted clearly and effectively, is among the most crucial of leadership traits.

It's never too late to improve your communication skills. Make the magnet of your words your signature. Invest in those skills, and you'll draw benefits until the very end of your lifetime journey.

Learn to take risks

Nurture within yourself the readiness to dare new things – to call on someone you don't know, to take on a task you've never tried before, to visit a new city or country, to work with people of a very different background from your own. Work yourself out of your comfort zone. Taking chances opens doors and creates lasting opportunities.

Risk is the spice of life's journey – and a meal without spice is bland and uninteresting.

Of course, it's important to understand the risks you take beforehand. Take risks with your eyes wide open. Make sure you do the research necessary to grasp fully both the upside and the downside of any choice you are considering. When presented with options by a colleague or adviser, always ask, 'What risks are involved?' You'll find that, quite often, this information is *not* volunteered – you have to ask for it. And believe me, there are *always* risks involved, however modest. At the very least, there is always the 'opportunity risk' involved in choosing any path – because taking Path A means, by definition, that you must pass up the opportunity to explore Path B, Path C and Path D.

Being aware of the risks you are taking shouldn't paralyse you; it should simply help you choose the risks you want to accept and avoid those that are too far beyond your tolerance. Awareness also makes it possible for you to look for ways to reduce those risks or even transform them into strengths.

One reason many people hesitate to take risks is an inordinate fear of failure. I've already spoken about 'the sweet taste of failure' and the fact that our inevitable setbacks create opportunities for learning and growth. Thinking about failure this way should help you reduce your anxiety about it and increase your confidence level with risk taking.

However, I would go further. I would say that many young people need to discover that the game of life is not exclusively about winning or losing. Those things are important, of course. In work and in life, you want to strive for excellence at all times – and when you do that, you'll experience the joy of victory more often than not, whether as an individual (through pay increases, promotions and the respect of your colleagues) or as part of an organization (through growth, profits and satisfied customers). There's no doubt about it – winning is sweet!

Nevertheless, I've lived long enough to realize that winning and losing are both fleeting, transitory experiences. No one wins or loses every time. That means today's victory or defeat, no matter how important, cannot be your sole or most important legacy. What matters more than winning or losing is how you play the game. This is your mark – what people will remember about you – and it is what shapes and prepares you for the next competition. And believe me, the next chance will come – if not today, then tomorrow or the day after that. But how the game is played showcases the full competency of your team and the organization, and this is for keeps.

Learn to focus a little less on today's score, whether winning or losing, and a little more on how you are shaping your talents, mind, spirit and soul, the power of your team, and the reputation of your organization through the way you play the game. With this attitude, you'll be better prepared to make wise decisions for the long run; you'll be less tempted to compromise your integrity for short-term gain; and you'll be better able to put risk in its proper perspective.

Innovate, don't imitate!

Many managers tend to think short-term and conventional rather than long-term and bold. This kind of 'me-too' thinking often leads to mediocrity. By contrast, a fearless commitment to innovation adds value to the organization, to those it serves, to shareholders and to society at large.

At B.I.G., we try to be pioneers in every business we participate in. We know that, if we continue to fish the same pond, we are bound to catch the same species. To achieve new things, we need to explore new territories – new product sources, new markets, new pools of talent, new customer bases and new business models. We've developed the habit of continually asking: What can we do differently? What can we improve? What new opportunity have we overlooked? This habit helps make innovation routine and second nature.

Organizational leaders need to develop the habit of scanning the playing field constantly. What are competitors doing that we can study – and transform? What is out there that is good but could be better? How can we create long-term, sustainable value through offerings that are genuinely innovative rather than imitative? After all, imitation is often cheaper than innovation and therefore tempting – but it is inherently perishable, a merely short-term solution to the value-creation challenge.

In my years in business, I've gotten to know many remarkable innovators. One of the most impressive was my friend, the late Ueli Prager, founder of the highly successful Mövenpick chain of hotels and resorts. Many years ago, Ueli and I built a hotel from scratch together located in Switzerland – half an hour from Basel, an hour from Zurich – in a beautiful spot that was then widely known as the busiest crossroads in Europe, viewed by 50,000 pairs of eyes every day.

Ueli built his hospitality business on the basis of a clear, simple, yet innovative vision of what customers really wanted – in particular, fresh, high-quality food served quickly and affordably for busy travellers. The name of his business reflected that insight: after spotting a diving seagull deftly plucking a fish from the water, Ueli vowed to make it just as simple for people on the go to 'move and pick' delicious meals from one of his restaurants, and so he dubbed his chain Mövenpick.

Ueli was one of the first restaurateurs in Europe to serve sandwiches and salads à la carte. He also made unusual design choices based on his deep understanding of customer psychology – for example, putting a bakery just inside the entrance to a hotel so that the enticing aroma of freshly-based bread would lure visitors into the building and through the doors of its nearby restaurant.

Although neither B.I.G. nor I are involved in the hospitality business today, I learned a great deal about creative thinking, human inter- actions, and business innovation from watching and speaking with Ueli Prager over the years. He will be greatly missed.

In many organizations, innovation occurs only when failure looms. People accept and even embrace change in such circumstances because they've been on the other side before – the dire consequences of the status quo – and they know it didn't work! At times like this, the leader's job is to find a way out of the swamp, offering a new vision that colleagues can rally around.

Fortunate organizations are gifted with leaders who don't wait for imminent failure to promote change. They recognize opportunities when they arise, help create innovations to realize them, and inspire those around them to embrace the change. In this way, they build success on success, reaching ever greater heights of achievement without having to experience the depths of failure.

Create your what-*not*-to-do list

Most people are familiar with the concept of a to-do list. It's a handy way to track and prioritize important tasks. But I believe that people who achieve the most in work and life also have a what-not-to-do list. It may be a real list, written on a piece of paper, or just a set of ideas that they live by. Either way, it's just as useful a tool as the traditional to-do list.

I formulated the idea of the what-not-to-do list after studying great companies and their leadership. One of the things I learned was that these companies routinely eliminated activities and pursuits that did not significantly contribute to the three most important criteria – the 'three Ps' of profit, passion and perfection.

Profit is about creating value, both for the company and for its customers. Passion is about having a noble purpose beyond just making money. Perfection is about focusing on flawlessly executing every task, so that the competition becomes less relevant. All three of these criteria must be met for a company to be truly great. In effect, they make up the long-term to-do list that great companies seem to share.

But what's easy to overlook is the fact that this to-do list of three important criteria must also be complemented by a list of activities to eliminate in order to free up time, energy, attention and resources for the three Ps – in short, a what-not-to-do list.

I think a similar philosophy applies to the individual. It's not hard to make a to-do list of important goals you want to achieve, whether in the next day, the next month, the next year or the next decade. Focusing your best efforts on these goals is absolutely essential if you hope to reach them, but it's just as important to clear away the activities that distract you, squander time and energy, waste money, and dissipate your focus on your real objectives.

Do you ever find yourself saying, 'I wish I could do X – but I just don't have the time'? X could be anything that is truly rewarding – getting more exercise, reading worthwhile books, taking a valuable class, mastering a new skill, completing an overdue project, improving your personal or professional relationships, or whatever. If you are in this familiar trap, take a few moments to list all the things you do every week that you don't *have* to do and that give you very little psychic, spiritual or physical reward. (Your list will be unique to you but, if you are like many people, time drains like watching TV, playing computer games and surfing the internet may be near the top.) Now imagine how many hours could be freed up if you were to eliminate (or even sharply reduce) those purposeless pursuits! Suddenly, 'doing X' no longer appears impossible. In fact, it may actually be easy – once you make the decision to act.

To help you identify the items for your what-not-to-do list, try something I call 'the 10–5 exercise'. Imagine you have just inherited $10 million, free and clear, to use exactly as you like – but with one condition: you have only five years in which to spend it in the pursuit of everlasting fulfilment. With the clock ticking, how would you change your life? What would you do differently? And just as important, what would you *stop* doing?

The 10–5 exercise is a striking way of identifying your *real* personal priorities – the things that truly matter to you in life. Those priorities are what deserve your focus and your energy; most of the rest is secondary at best.

So the next time you jot down your to-do list, take an extra step. Write a what-not-to-do list alongside it – and start putting it into practice immediately. Your chances of achieving the goals you've listed will go way, way up.

Seize every moment!

In today's ultra-competitive, constantly changing world, we are all travelling at a much faster pace than many of us think. In an environment that's moving at 100 miles per hour, for us to stay at the forefront we simply cannot afford to travel at just half that speed and lag behind. So do whatever it takes to enhance your own energy level. It may mean improving your diet, making time for daily exercise, cutting out time and energy wasters like television and computer games, or using meditation to enhance your relaxation and improve the quality of your rest. Speed up your own reflexes, and make the most of every week, every day and every hour.

In so many cases, what differentiates a problem from a disaster is simply *reaction time*. Moving quickly is not just about individual performance. It's also a basic principle of good leadership in today's world. In my role at B.I.G., I make a point of being firm about setting timetables and schedules, not just for myself but for the entire organization. 'We're not out for a weekend drive', I like to say to the members of my team. 'We're in a race – and we need to win!'

To encourage the same do-it-now attitude throughout B.I.G., we set limits on the tenure in office of key corporate leaders. For example, each member of our board serves a five-year term, renewable by mutual consent, rather than the unlimited lifetime tenure that is more typical in some parts of our region. The message this sends is quiet and respectful, but unmistakable: 'We're not going to be here for ever. So let's hit our goals now, not in some distant future.' The principle of the fiscal year as a measuring yardstick for accomplishment enforces the same function. The key question by which achievement is gauged is always 'What have we done this year?'

In the corporate world, we constantly need to drive our agenda with limited, specific timelines – because we don't have unlimited time in which to cruise along at our own speed. Remember, if you're not fast, you're food!

Don't rush the process of self-development

Strive to develop patience when it comes to your journey of self-discovery. Take the journey in thoughtful strides rather than trying to make one or two giant leaps to the top. Climb the career ladder consistently, step by step, without seeking short cuts, and remembering to pause for reflection. Otherwise, you may find you've vaulted to the top of the *wrong* ladder, reaching career milestones that turn out to be unfulfilling.

Seek to master the art of self-discipline. Learn how your mind works, and the tricks it will play on you – and develop the willpower to do what you need to do despite those tricks. For example, if you start a daily exercise routine, you'll probably experience a moment when your mind whispers to you, 'Come on – you don't really want to exercise today, do you? Aren't you tired?' Now, most of us today don't work at jobs that are physically exhausting, so when our mind tells us we are 'tired' it is really the brain itself that is tired – and is trying to trick us into going along for the easy ride.

At this point, you have a choice. You can yield to your impulse, put off exercise, and find that exercising becomes harder and harder to do. Or you can simply ignore the mind's whispering and head for the gym. If you do the latter, you'll find, after 15 minutes or so on the cross-trainer, that you're actually *not* tired – and that exercising is making you feel stronger and more energetic.

The lesson: you can strengthen your willpower through exercise, just like any other muscle – provided you're prepared to ignore the mind and the tricks it will play on you. The same philosophy applies not just to working out but to any other form of self-discipline, from working hard and doing your homework to controlling the urge to indulge in life's extreme temptations.

When confronted with a daunting task, don't waste time standing at the base of the mountain fretting about how high the peak is and how tough the climb will be. Start climbing! There will be plenty of time during the journey to look back and gain perspective on how far you've come.

Don't approach life with a service station mentality – as if it's about getting a periodic fill-up from an attendant with little or no effort on your part. Instead, take on the farmer's mentality. Start with well-chosen seeds, prepare the soil, plant, water, nurture, fertilize, and harvest with care. When you develop these skills, you create an annual rhythm that produces consistent benefits for everyone.

Never forget the danger of hubris. A little success often leads to conceit and a refusal to listen and learn. This is especially dangerous in a society with a tradition of conservative, top-down leadership, and it's one reason some people with the potential to be leaders fall short. Truth doesn't hurt – it's the sudden realization of truth that hurts! Don't allow arrogance to blind you to the truth. Fight the tendency to become smug or complacent.

We all have egos, of course. But with success the power of the ego can pose a real danger. What do I do with my ego every day? I make sure it is locked in a jar called 'humility' before I walk out the door.

Finally, as you prepare to embark on your lifetime journey, think of yourself as a sculpture that remains unfinished – one that is continually being refined and improved as a result of life lessons and experiences. What matters is not completing the sculpture, but rather continually enhancing it – and never being satisfied with 'good enough'.

4

The six qualities of a true leader

At the end of every journey, we look for signs and signals that we've arrived. If true leadership is your goal, how will you know when you've reached your destination? What are the distinguishing signs and signals that mark a true leader?

One distinction that it is important to make is between leadership and authority. Authority is bestowed upon you. It comes by virtue of a title, a position or an official designation. Leadership, by contrast, grows from within. It is a set of characteristics that define the kind of person others rally around, listen to, look to for guidance, and accept as a role model.

In some cases, authority and leadership are separated. When the person with authority lacks leadership, the organization suffers. Success and improvement are elusive. Unless a true leader emerges to keep the organization on track, it may fail altogether. Without leadership, no business, non-profit organization, academic institution, government body or any other kind of organization can thrive.

Ideally, however, authority and leadership should go together – and in many well-run organizations they do. The best organizations have powerful leaders in positions of authority, as well as many other individuals with strong leadership traits scattered throughout the ranks. Some of these Unknown Leaders will eventually rise to their own positions of authority, while others may remain in more modest roles, quietly exerting the power of leadership to enhance the quality, productivity and integrity of everyone around them.

If you are currently in a position of authority, congratulations – you've been given an important responsibility for the future of your organization and the people whose lives it touches. Now you must make sure you are developing your leadership qualities to the utmost, so that you can live up to the responsibility you've been given.

If you are not yet in a position of authority, now is the time to start your journey of self-discovery. It's a journey of preparation, aimed at discovering your leadership capacities and developing them fully. You want to be ready for the moment – it may arrive tomorrow or 10 years from today – when you are called upon to lead, when the future of your organization lies wholly or partially in your hands.

But this still leaves unanswered the crucial question: What, *exactly*, is this elusive quality we call leadership? Is it possible to define and describe it in specific language?

Recently, we at Banawi Industrial Group decided to offer an annual award to honour some of our country's most remarkable young leaders in the private sector. In planning the award process, we realized we needed a clear definition of 'leadership' in order to have consistent criteria for the prize. This led to a prolonged, lively and thoughtful conversation among my associates within and outside B.I.G. and myself about what leadership really means. How do we recognize leadership in one another – and in ourselves?

We soon came to the conclusion that leadership is not a single, discrete characteristic or way of behaving, but rather a complex collection of traits whose interaction and combination give birth to effective behaviour in a wide range of challenging situations. If leadership were a simple matter, it could be reduced to a formula: 'Do this'; 'Say that'; 'Follow these steps.' However, the problems we face in life and work are rarely simple and predictable. They are complicated and challenging, and they have consequences and ramifications that are difficult to foresee, so the leadership traits required to make the right decisions can't be captured in a simple guide. Instead, they are nuanced, complicated qualities that take time and effort to develop and a lifetime to perfect, and which every great leader expresses in a unique and personal fashion.

Our debate and the search that followed, together with the lessons learned from my own lifetime journey, made me believe that the following list of six attributes captures the crucial characteristics of a leader. A true leader is:

- **visionary;**

- **authentic;**

- **nurturing;**

- **collaborative;**

- **resilient;**

- **committed to excellence in execution.**

These words are rich in implication – but what do they really mean? Let's take some time to unpack each one and explain how it works in practice.

Visionary

I define a vision as 'a dream with precise architecture' – one that is capable of inspiring others to join the quest of bringing the dream to reality. Leaders with a sound sense of tactics are plentiful; those who are able to project a vision for the long term are uncommon and therefore much more valuable. Such leaders don't just create opportunities – they leave behind institutions and a thriving corporate culture that bring out the best in individuals and teams.

There is an element of benevolence in a vision that separates it from a 'grand scheme'. True visionaries consider all their constituencies as full-fledged stakeholders in their vision. A vision is not elitist, but rather built on inclusiveness. It embraces and empowers those around us in ways that help them develop and realize their own visions.

The soul of a vision is always about improving the quality of life for individual men and women. Without this selfless cause, a vision is inadequate and lacking. Even as they tackle the countless details that must be done right to realize the vision, leaders must remain true to its soul – because only the soul of the vision has the power to truly inspire.

A vision never comes with a guarantee, but if it is inspirational and binding it can attract others to join you on the journey, making the realization of the vision a matter of time. Visions may even survive the visionaries themselves and be within our grasp only after the visionaries' passing. A visionary is like the first runner in a relay race, handing the baton on to successors who are inspired by the example to reach the ultimate finish line. Thus a vision is often more far-reaching and all-encompassing than the individual who first articulated it.

The scope and breadth of a vision can vary greatly, from one that may change the history of a nation, a region or even the world to one that is much more modest yet daring and still very significant for the people affected by it. For example, recall the vision for Dubai as a dynamic economic regional hub for the entire Middle East, created under the leadership of Sheikh Mohammed, as we explained it in Chapter 2. The remarkable transformation of Dubai from an ordinary city on the map just a few years ago into a vibrant, progressive hub unlike any other in the world while still holding to its high tradition and heritage demonstrates the phenomenal power of a vision brought to life. When you visit Dubai today, you can see that much of this vision has already been realized and more is on the way. As this vision comes to complete fruition over the decades ahead, it will enrich the lives of millions of people in many countries, creating a holistic climate for job opportunities while building complementary industries and diversifying the regional economy.

In most cases, a big vision like this one includes smaller component parts – what you might call 'subvisions' – that others may envision and help to realize. In this way, the great vision launched by one person or group of people may come to inspire thousands or even millions of other people to contribute through personal visions of their own. The jobs that some people may think of as trivial or unimportant are often simply the small wheels that make the big wheels turn – without which no great vision can come to fruition.

History provides a range of examples of visions with epic scope. In 1961, when President John F Kennedy challenged the United States 'to achieving the goal, before this decade is out, of landing a man on the moon and returning him safely to the earth', he articulated an ambitious vision that many considered impossible. His vision ultimately harnessed the efforts of thousands of individuals and was successfully realized with the historic moon landing of July 1969 – even when President Kennedy himself was no longer alive to witness it.

An inspiring vision can also be much more modest, designed on a far smaller scale. Everyone has the opportunity to have a vision – not just company founders, national leaders or others who are officially anointed as 'leaders'. For example, as we saw in Chapter 1, Dr Asma Siddiki has created an inspiring vision of learning programmes that will provide young people with a deeper understanding of and appreciation for the cultural heritage of their homelands. It is a vision that started with a simple idea in the mind of a young woman, and was launched with a modest pilot programme involving just nine students. Now it is growing, and some day soon it may touch the lives of hundreds or even thousands of individuals – a great tree of learning, growing from a single tiny seed.

At first glance, the vision for Dubai developed by Sheikh Mohammed may seem to have little in common with the vision for Heritage Summers that Dr Asma Siddiki is building. One is a complex series of government-sponsored private–public mega-projects designed to transform the economy of an entire region, bringing new prosperity to millions of people; the other is a new kind of educational pro-gramme, the brainchild of one highly motivated woman, intended to help a select group of curious young people gain a richer understanding of their own cultural heritage. Yet both qualify as inspiring visions – vividly detailed plans that excite people with a glimpse of a better world and make them eager to participate and contribute.

Inspiring visions can take many forms. If you are an entrepreneur, your vision may be to create the finest business of its kind in your neighbourhood or city. If you are a young manager, it may be to climb the corporate ladder to the high ranks of exceptional leader-ship. If you are a public servant, it may be to make your agency a model of efficiency, integrity and effectiveness. As consumers, we see familiar and powerful brands of products and services all around us, whether on shelves of stores or in services that are integral to our daily lives. Behind each and every one of these goods and services and the corporations that bring them to us is a vision worthy of admiration.

Powerful visions are also found outside the world of business. If you are a school principal, your vision may be to inspire every child in every class with the desire to attend college or university and pursue a challenging career. If you are a student, it may be to design and execute a futuristic research project that will stretch the limits of your talents and knowledge. If you are a parent, it may be to raise a family of self-confident young people who combine 21st-century skills with the best values and work ethic. All of these visions are worthy goals that are capable of inspiring intense creative effort for years to come.

As I've already indicated, a vision is not a vague daydream. Its 'precise architecture' is essential to making the vision a reality. The visionary leader isn't content simply to imagine a better world, but is fixated on making the vision real, and devotes a lifetime to the pursuit of the vision by developing winning strategies and mastering the crucial details. At the same time, the visionary leader does not become submerged in the details, but retains a firm grasp on the broader picture so that the inspiring soul of the vision is never lost.

The precise architecture of the vision also includes the diversity of talents necessary to contribute to its realization. If the vision is blurry, then the search for talent will be blurry – and the results will be disappointing.

Think of talent as the 'human software' required to make the vision come true. This software may take many forms and may be housed in individuals whose backgrounds, personalities and styles vary widely. This is one reason a true leader cherishes diversity.

It's natural to surround oneself with people who are similar to you or whom you like personally. The visionary leader is not content with this approach. Instead, leaders focus, laser-like, on the demands of the vision. They attract people with talents they don't themselves possess, including even people they may find uncongenial for personal reasons. Leaders know that, when pursuing a vision, the extent to which you personally like the people who support that vision matters little. If the essential integrity and skills are present, along with commitment to the vision, then such people should become part of the team – because what is most important is realizing the vision.

If you are an aspiring leader, ask yourself: what kind of vision can I create? Don't be afraid to think big. And when you are starting your career and considering your job options, study the corporate vision of any enterprise you are thinking about joining. Ask yourself: does this vision give me goosebumps? If the answer is yes, that's the company you should be associated with. This way, you will never have to think of work as just work, but as a milestone in your life-long journey.

If you can craft a vision that is inspiring and then develop the precise architecture required to make the dream a reality – without ever losing sight of its soul – you may have the makings of a true leader.

Authentic

Real leaders are true to their principles, willing to admit mistakes and accept responsibility, and capable of emerging whole and sound when tested. Authenticity is a particular signature of real leaders – a connecting thread that makes every step in their life journey into a unified whole. It brings all the other qualities of leaders together in a satisfying combination, just as a special spice or a distinct herb can create harmony among the various ingredients that give a meal a memorable flavour. Authentic leaders are able to connect with others so the others are eager to embrace the message and vision.

When we think of leaders who have inspired millions to join great causes, we usually think of men and women of deep authenticity – leaders like Mahatma Gandhi, with his profound personal commitment to Indian independence and non-violent resistance; Nelson Mandela, who sacrificed 27 years in prison before seeing his vision of a free, multiracial South Africa realized; and Saudi Arabia's King Faisal, who in the sixties selflessly championed the early modernization of the Kingdom.

When I interview job candidates, I like to ask, 'Tell me your life story. Explain how one experience led to the next and what it all means.' I am often surprised by the number of candidates who are unable to explain how the various things they have done fit together; sometimes they are unwilling to acknowledge mistakes or to take responsibility for their choices.

By contrast, true leaders welcome having their decisions scrutinized and tested. They understand that a failure of decision is not necessarily a failure of character, and that every mistake is an opportunity to learn and grow. This understanding, too, is an aspect of the authenticity that is a hallmark of the leader.

Authenticity is closely intertwined with integrity and ethics. People who are authentic are unafraid to reveal their true selves – and this can be the case only when they feel sure that they have done what is right according to their best lights, rather than fudging the truth, cutting moral corners or taking advantage of ambiguity to benefit themselves at the expense of others. We often describe people of integrity by saying 'They have nothing to hide', and the expression highlights the transparency that goes with integrity and depends upon it.

Thus, if you find yourself, at any point in your career, feeling the need to 'put on an act' or wear a mask in the presence of colleagues, rivals, customers or the general public, stop and take the time to examine your conscience. Perhaps you are experiencing, just below the surface, the feeling of remorse that arises from knowing that your behaviour has not been morally spotless – that you have done something you are not proud of or done some injustice to others in order to benefit yourself.

The sure way to avoid this feeling of remorse is to become accustomed, from the very beginning of your career, to considering the ethical dimensions of every choice you make, elevating these to the very highest standard in your decision-making process, and avoiding the temptations of self-interest at the expense of others.

We all know that business takes place in a highly competitive arena. Rivalries between individuals and companies are often intense. Strong feelings arise. But tough business battles and struggles to get ahead shouldn't mean compromising your integrity.

When you have to fight, fight up, not down. Even if adversaries resort to questionable tactics, don't stoop to their level. Fight with honour. Then you will be proud to live by the outcome, whether you win or lose.

Integrity doesn't only mean avoiding wrongdoing. It also means living by your word – keeping your promises, meeting or beating deadlines, under-promising and over-delivering. These, too, are closely linked with authenticity. Authentic leaders are those whose words and actions are one and the same. They exemplify in their own behaviour the values that they publicly espouse and ask their colleagues and followers to subscribe to and practise. In time, these values become second nature to them.

The importance of congruence between your words and your actions means that you must think carefully before you speak. Pause and be sure you know what you're talking about before you make a promise or commitment.

Nurturing

True leadership is about nurturing others – about helping those around you to achieve their fullest potential, without thinking about whether you will benefit in the process. It is not about the benefits that flow to the leader, such as wealth, fame, perks and prestige. Fundamental to being a leader is to give more than you take every day of your professional life.

The art of leadership-as-nurturing takes several forms. Leaders are a source of knowledge on a relentless search for more. They keep learning throughout their lives, and delight at every chance to pass knowledge and experience on to others. Real leaders are also gifted with the patience to allow others to grow and explore. To be nurturing requires control over one's own ego, and remembering that the role of the leader is ultimately to serve.

Here is a small example of how I try to practise the principle of nurturing in my everyday work as a leader. I call it 'filling the gaps'. As each work day draws to a close, I take a moment to reflect on my personal interactions for that day. Is there someone I may have inadvertently offended? Did I brush off someone's concerns because of time pressure, inattention or a momentary distraction? If so, I pick up the phone or write an e-mail to clear the air immediately rather than leaving it hanging. In most cases, a simple message – a sincere apology or a word of encouragement or explanation – is all it takes to lay the foundation for a positive and productive tomorrow. Doing this is easy; what marks the nurturing leader is the simple commitment to practise it, day in and day out.

It's ironic: in nurturing others, leaders often discover that giving to others leads to enormous personal growth. When leaders try to 'save' someone who needs their guidance, support and mentoring, they often discover that they themselves are the ones being saved, becoming better and more fulfilled people in the process of helping another. We should be ever grateful for opportunities like this to have our minds opened, capable of seeing the inside of life as well as the outside!

A nurturing style of leadership can be applied in a wide range of situations. My friend Nabil Alyousuf, whose story I recounted in Chapter 2, faced his first major leadership challenge at the tender age of 23. As I've explained, Nabil was given the chance to run a textile mill on behalf of the investment bank he worked for, which had a majority ownership stake in the mill. He found that he had to develop an effective leadership style that would lead to the greatest productivity on the part of the mill workers, many of whom were unskilled or semi-skilled labourers from South-East Asia and Pakistan.

Nabil explains:

> *The conventional management style in the textile industry is authoritarian and demeaning, designed to squeeze as much as you can out of the workers. The logic says these people are used to this, that this is the way they've been accustomed to being treated their whole life, and that if you treat them well they will stop working hard or may even be defiant. But this harsh approach to leadership didn't fit my nature, so I didn't practise it at all. In fact, I did the opposite. I would visit the mill, talk to all of the workers, ask them about their problems and needs, and try hard to deal with each person fairly. I had an open-door policy and encouraged any worker with an issue to come to me to discuss it.*

> *The discovery I made is that, if you treat people well, they will work hard for you and give you their loyalty. In fact, I was able to get much more work from the same people than their own countrymen did using the traditional harsh methods, and I even received much more loyalty from them, despite being from a completely different culture. So treating people in a caring, nurturing fashion has become a hallmark of my leadership style. The textile mill was where I first realized how effective it can be.*

For many leaders, it is easy to remember to be nurturing to the people we work with every day – our immediate colleagues, those we report to and those who report directly to us. As you rise through the ranks, it may be harder to remember to nurture those who are on the lower rungs of the organization as Nabil describes, but everyone who contributes to the success of our efforts is important and deserving of our nurturing support. One mark of true leaders is that they never forget this essential truth.

Collaborative

In today's complex world, the traditional model of top-down, autocratic leadership simply won't work. Realizing any organizational vision requires in-depth understanding and the ability to make smart, informed decisions at every level in the organization and at every step in the process. In short, today's world demands co-pilots, not just followers – and this means that the leader must be prepared to lead in a collaborative rather than authoritarian style.

Leaders evolve by keeping in touch; they are connected through mind and soul receptors that are switched on all the time. They pick up signals from anyone and at every juncture. They value a word or a thought of an ordinary person, because they understand that brilliance often starts as a simple seed that finds the right soil, the right climate and the right care to emerge and grow.

Effective leadership instils confidence and dispels doubt. It allows controversy and welcomes diversity; it invites innovation and provokes creativity. It is sometimes critical, but never cynical.

Collaboration requires courage on the part of both leaders and co-workers. After all, the only way a co-pilot can be trained to respond in an emergency is by frequently taking the wheel and guiding the aircraft – and this means that the pilot must be prepared to trust and support the co-pilot, even when he makes the occasional beginner's mistake.

Collaboration also requires openness to ideas that originate anywhere in the organization. A real leader is able to bring together people with differing ideas and help them work towards consensus in the service of the overarching vision. Disagreement, I've found, is like cement – when it's fresh, it's soft and can be easily reshaped; in time, it hardens and becomes inflexible. The true leader flushes out disagreements and clears the air early rather than letting them linger.

It's easy for leaders to *prevent* this kind of collaboration by rushing to judgement or short-circuiting discussions before alternative points of view have been aired. A true leader has the self-confidence to allow open debate rather than fearing the disagreements or conflicts that may arise. In Chapter 1, I described the experience of working with Ghazi Binzagr on the governor's think tank on the vision for the Medinah region. This was an example of the power of creative dialogue to foster collaboration and innovation. When people are allowed to 'lock horns' in a beneficial, mutually respectful fashion, ideas get reframed so as to address others' concerns. The result is not a mere mechanical exchange of positions but rather a creative synthesis, opening doors to new insights and imaginative break-throughs no individual could hope to achieve alone.

Finally, the collaborative leader is ready to accept the responsibility when things go wrong, but quick to share the triumph when things go well. When people know they will receive credit for their contri-butions, they are eager to help support your cause; and when they know they will not be left 'hanging out to dry' in times of trouble, they will stand by your side, giving you the same kind of devotion you've given to them.

Collaborative leadership makes every member of an organization stronger. A primary measure of the value we bring to our world is the degree to which those around us become better people through their association with us – people of greater principles, character and mettle. When you want to know your own value, look at those who have been around you throughout your life. Their value is your value!

Resilient

Examine the life stories of real leaders and you'll be startled to see how often they have been written off in times of trouble. The real leader understands that winning and losing are not the crucial test of leadership. As every world-class athlete knows, the contender who wins today is likely to lose tomorrow, and vice versa. The crucial issue is how resilient you are – how ready you are to bounce back from defeat with renewed energy and resolve. Tested by adversity, either personal or professional, a leader is prepared to withstand future challenges with authenticity, grace, humility, strength and endurance. In times of triumph, a leader is wise enough to avoid excessive celebration, which may lead to a state of euphoria and the illusions that go with it.

When the world seems to be collapsing around you, it's easy to give in to despair – to panic, break down, become filled with anger, or blame those around you. Resilient leaders resist this temptation. They control their emotions, communicating optimism even when the clouds above are darkest – because they know that the emotions of the leader are contagious and will quickly spread to the entire organization.

The strength of the leader has a way of permeating the entire organization. When the leader is resilient, so is the organization. It is this balance of character, this so-called temperament, that distinguishes those who exercise true leadership from those who merely exercise authority.

Of course, resilience is not just a matter of temperament. It also requires the leader to have a steady hand and exercise good judge-ment in tough times and turmoil. When we face setbacks, we look to the leader for answers – a safe passage out of the storm. The leader is someone who is expected to steer the organization and its people through rough terrain into greener pasture.

MAHA AL-GHUNAIM
Resilience in the eye of the storm

Maha Al-Ghunaim is one of the most successful Arab women in an industry that has relatively few notable female leaders, in the Middle East or anywhere else in the world – international banking and investment management.

I was fortunate enough to meet Maha at an important moment in the history of our company. Back in 2006, B.I.G. was considering its future options for growth. As part of this process, we entered into conversations with Global Investment House – the Kuwait-based investment firm that Maha Al-Ghunaim had co-founded and served as chair person and managing director – about making an investment in B.I.G. The discussion went well, and a deal seemed to be looming until – as often happens – our working teams found themselves at odds over the proper valuation of B.I.G. for the funds the company manages. They began to dig in their heels; emotions began getting in the way of working out the snags.

I surprised my advisers by suggesting that I fly to Kuwait to meet with Maha face to face. Then, when we arrived, I surprised them further by proposing a one-to-one conversation between the two of us – no lawyers, accountants or other negotiators in the room. My feeling was that we needed to wring the emotions out of the discussion, and that sometimes having extra people around the table can heighten and intensify the emotions rather than calming them.

Our meeting was very cordial and straightforward. I told Maha, 'Your reputation precedes you as a woman who exercises leadership through integrity and fair play. These are similar values to those I work hard to instil and nourish within the corporate culture of B.I.G.' I explained that both companies shared the belief that a business partnership must always be more than a mere transaction. 'If it's the right thing for both of us that this deal should go through', I told her, 'then we should make it happen, and not let details throw us off course.'

Maha agreed that our corporate values were similar, and that she wanted Global to be part of the B.I.G. story. 'Let me go over this with my team during the next week', she said. We called in both teams and told them we had agreed on a way forward.

A week later, after conferring with her team, she called me, and we cut a deal over the phone. Our sense of mutual respect and trust was solidified, and I suspect it will never go away.

Since then, with changes in business conditions, B.I.G. has bought back its shares from Global, ending our financial partnership, at least temporarily, but both companies view this not as a divorce but as a mutually supportive parting of the ways, with the understanding that each of us has an ally in the other for the future.

I'm not the only business person who has developed a deep respect for Maha Al-Ghunaim. Many others share my opinion of her – and I think that, once you've heard her story, you'll understand why I consider her one of our region's most admirable leaders. She is well recognized in the financial and investment communities in the region and beyond, but I consider her a worthy role model for Unknown Leaders because of the extraordinary qualities she exhibited in a 'perfect storm' of business difficulties, surviving with renewed resolve to tell the story.

After graduating from San Francisco State University in California with a degree in mathematics, Maha Al-Ghunaim was hired by an investment firm run by the government of Kuwait. Offered a choice among several departments, including the treasury department, the credit department and the marketable securities department (which dealt in stocks and bonds), she chose the last one, reasoning that, 'As an individual investor, marketable securities is how I could build my own wealth – so that is what I want to learn about.' At that time, in the late 1980s, Maha was one of just a very few women working in that field.

She started her career on the bottom rung of the ladder: 'I worked as a clerk with a calculator and a huge ledger book, adding and subtracting numbers all day.' She also faced considerable scepticism from colleagues who assumed she wasn't serious about her career – that as an attractive young woman from a prosperous family she must be working just to pass time until she got married. Maha ignored the critical comments: 'I really didn't care. I loved what I was doing! And so I worked extra hard, until the people around me were forced to admit that I knew what I was doing, and that I was doing what everyone expected of me plus a little bit more.'

Soon she was promoted to investment dealer, one of the first women ever to hold that very responsible post. Here she thrived, because her fascination with finding investment ideas and her readiness to devote long hours to research and analysis enabled her to come up with deals that made the firm a lot of money – and, as Maha says, 'When the results can be measured in hard numbers, no one can deny that they are real and that respect has been earned.' Clients whose funds Maha helped to multiply quickly learned to appreciate her insights.

By 1998, Maha had begun to chafe under the restrictions of working in a government-run investment firm, and she and a few close colleagues decided to launch their own company – Global Investment House. Thanks to the excellent reputation she had developed and the close bonds she had forged with a number of clients, they raised all the capital they needed within just two weeks – a remarkable accomplishment.

For almost a decade, Global thrived. Starting from a modest $50 million base, it grew into an enterprise valued at $5 billion, with assets under management totalling over $10 billion by mid 2008. Its shares were listed on the public exchanges in Kuwait, Bahrain, Dubai and London – in fact, it was the only Kuwaiti company listed in London. At the height of the market, $1 million invested with Maha had grown in value to $60 million. 'I thought we were on top of the world', Maha says.

And then the global financial crisis of 2008 hit. Practically every financial company in the world was affected. Those that had been managed with great conservatism (and so had grown only modestly) were affected least; those that had been more aggressive and taken greater risks (and therefore grown spectacularly) were hit more severely. Global was among the latter. As assets plummeted in value, credit lines dried up, depriving her company (and others like it) of the funds they relied on to operate. 'It was like having a beautiful Ferrari with an excellent driver – but without oil', Maha recalls. 'There was nothing we could do about it.' Global defaulted on its debt in December 2008. It was the kind of blow that many financial firms never recover from – a brutal test of Maha's resiliency as a leader.

Public perceptions worsened Global's crisis. As it had received worldwide media acclaim during its period of ascendancy, Global's position as one of the first financial firms to report serious credit problems during the financial meltdown caused some observers to turn against it and against Maha, accusing her of mismanagement, incompetence or worse. (When many other firms suffered similar difficulties, the personal attacks on Maha and Global lessened – but that didn't happen for almost a year.)

Meanwhile, Maha and her leadership team had to take a series of difficult, painful steps. Panicky clients and shareholders had to be mollified; the need for transparency in the crisis forced Global's senior management to explain their strategic missteps in excruciating, humbling detail. Recognizing the need for knowledge of a kind they didn't possess, they brought in debt restructuring experts to help negotiate new arrangements with Global's bank creditors. (After agonizingly complex negotiations, 100 per cent of Global's 53 bank partners in countries around the world signed on to the settlement, a remarkable achievement in itself.) And of course, draconian internal changes were necessary. Employee bonuses were cancelled, pay increases were eliminated, and long-time members of staff were made redundant. Fortunately, Maha had the support and commitment of her best team members to stay the course rather than jump to the apparent safety of another firm. But over a three-year period, half the employees of Global lost their jobs.

As of early 2012, the global investment climate remains unsettled. The worst turmoil of 2009 seems to be behind us, but fresh crises seem to pop up every month, from the downgrade of US, European and Greek debt to political unrest in the Middle East. Like many financial firms, Global is still operating in a far more conservative manner than it did in the high-flying era of the early 2000s, waiting and hoping for investor confidence and business growth to reappear. The company has also dramatically changed its business model. It no longer invests its own funds in principal investments, and instead is focusing on less lucrative but more reliable fee-based services: investment banking, asset management, and brokerage.

All these adjustments – most of them painful – have posed enormous challenges for Maha, the leader at the eye of the storm. She observes:

> *In a time of crisis, people need to hear from you. As the leader, your job is to communicate confidence to them, even when things are bleak, and you do that using every method that you can think of. People watch you from the minute you walk in the door, reading messages into what you're wearing, what you look like, what kind of mood you are in. I'm known to have a very loud laugh, and some of my senior managers tell me that, when they hear me laugh, it's like a security blanket, telling them that things are all right because I am still here.*

When the world seems to be collapsing around you, it's easy to give in to despair – to panic, break down, become filled with anger, or blame those around you for the trouble. Resilient leaders resist this temptation. They find a way to control their emotions, communicating optimism even when the clouds are blackest overhead – because they know that the emotions of the leader are contagious and will quickly spread to the entire organization.

Resilient leaders have the strength to 'take one for the team'. Maha observes:

In times of good performance, you like to give credit to your team. That's how loyalty is built. But in bad times, the leader has to stand tall and take the blame. If you don't – if you try to deflect blame on to the people who work for you – you lose their trust and confidence. It's painful to accept responsibility in public for a disastrous situation, but it's one of the jobs made for true leaders.

Maha attributes her resilience in this prolonged period of crisis to two things. One is the help she received from her family and husband – in particular, his reminding her about the importance of separating the things that really matter from the things that don't:

There were so many rumours and attacks in the media, all of which I used to take very personally. It seems to be a rule that the bad noise is always louder than the good noise. My husband helped me realize that I only need to care about the opinions of those that matter to me, whether those I do business with or the members of my family, and that I need to tune out the distracting noise of outside criticism, especially when it's uninformed. Removing all that negative stress from my life released a lot of pressure and enabled me to focus on the important things rather than being defensive all the time.

The other source of strength has been Maha's faith: 'One of the most important supports for me is that I'm religious. That doesn't mean that I'm all covered up and praying all day and night. But being a Muslim and believing in my heart in the value of good karma, good actions and belief in God gave me a lot of spiritual strength during this crisis.'

Maha's resilience has not only enabled her to keep going through difficult times, but also inspired those around her to continue to believe in her company and its mission. One of her proudest possessions is a plaque presented to her by her senior management team in the midst of the financial crisis, on which they all pledged to continue to work for Global *without salary* if necessary. Maha tells me that none of the senior team have left except those who were asked to leave. It's quite a tribute to the loyalty that Maha's leadership attracts.

True leadership shines in adversity. One defining quality of leadership is that, when leaders have been considered 'history', they come back stronger than before, with their vision redefined, their authenticity more genuine, their nurturing instincts deepened, and all their other leadership traits more mature.

Committed to excellence in execution

Last, but certainly not least, real leaders are 'execution animals', driven by achievement. True leaders autograph their work with excellence and are constantly seeking opportunities to raise the bar of quality for the entire organization. By contrast, mediocrity is a malaise – one that we can choose to accept or reject. Sadly, far too many people are willing to settle for it rather than insisting on aiming high and working fiercely towards excellence.

There are lots of excuses for failure – but seldom a good reason – especially when you consider that good quality and poor quality generally take similar amounts of time to deliver.

Excellence in execution is not something the leader can delegate to others in its entirety and then walk away. You can't simply mandate high standards and then rely on others to achieve them. If you aspire to leadership, you must be personally dedicated to excellence and take the lead in achieving it.

This is one reason why a period of hands-on apprenticeship in the lower ranks of an organization is a useful, even essential, background for the leader. You need to spend some time personally mastering the skills that are crucial to success in your industry. If you work in manufacturing, put in some days on the assembly line; if you help to run a service business, devote time to working face to face with customers and learning about their needs and problems; if you are involved in health care, spend afternoons with patients and their families so you can understand what it takes to reassure and comfort them. If you haven't personally tried to meet the highest standards in your field, it will be hard for you to judge the performance of your colleagues, or to inspire them to give their best efforts in pursuit of excellence. Personal knowledge and hands-on experience provide credibility and credentials.

Of course, delegation is an important skill. No one person can do everything, so leaders must learn how to delegate effectively. They must give their colleagues not just a set of tasks to perform, but also ownership of the results – that is, a sense of personal responsibility for what happens. (I've found that, if you get the ownership of a task right, you usually get the resolution right.) Leaders must also give people enough freedom to develop their own solutions to knotty problems. This is the only way to nurture creativity, independent judgement, and responsibility among those who may be leading the entire organization some day.

The art of delegation is very important, but delegation mustn't occur at the expense of involvement by the leader. Even after you rise to a high level in the organization and are no longer personally required to perform certain tasks, it's a good idea to retain the 'hands-on' mindset – to stay directly involved in the execution of whatever broad strategy or plan you commit to. In particular, you must avoid delegating the key levers of the organization – those factors that are crucial to success or failure. Every organization defines those levers differently, based on the nature of the business and the competitive advantage of the organization. Leaders must constantly have their hands on these key levers and avoid excessive delegation of them. Of these, excellence in execution is often the most important.

Stay in touch and never abdicate the cycle of execution. Even the best plans may unravel when a leader does not keep a close watch. Even highly talented people can let their quality standards slip a bit when they feel that the boss isn't really engaged. There's no substitute for actually seeing, with your own eyes, what is happening on the ground, and for asking the hard questions that will enable you to judge the quality of the work that is being done.

In my current role as chairman and CEO of B.I.G., I work with a diverse group of talented professional colleagues with specialized skills in many areas – product design, research and development, engineering, manufacturing, information technology, supply chain, marketing and so on. Many of them have advanced knowledge about their specific areas of expertise that I will never be able to match, but I find there's a unique value in my staying in touch with the market-place personally. For example, when I travel throughout the region, I like to visit supermarkets and other stores where B.I.G.'s products may be on display. Among other things, we produce packaging solu-tions that are used by many leading consumer goods companies. Fairly often, my 'outsider's' eye spots an opportunity that our local team members haven't noticed. On a recent visit to Morocco, I scanned the shelves containing toothpastes and soaps, and I noticed that competing manufacturers seemed to dominate those categories. I told our divisional leaders about my observations and asked a few relevant questions. They're now taking a closer look at the market to see where the lost opportunities are and what we need to do to move B.I.G. to the top of the list of preferred suppliers for those potential customers.

Here's another example. B.I.G.'s speciality chemicals division pro-duces, among other materials, a number of adhesives that are widely used in consumer products. We like to say 'We're the matchmakers of industry', since our adhesives help to make a practical bond between two or more manufactured items. We pride ourselves on the consistent quality and reliability of our adhesives, so when I visit a retail store and I notice that the straw on a beverage container has fallen to the floor, or spot the label on a bottle of mineral water peeling off from one corner, or notice juice leaking from the corner of a package, I'll send a message to the appropriate executive with the name of the product.

'Here's an adhesive that's not performing the way it should', I'll say. 'Please check who the supplier is. I hope and trust it is not us.' If the flawed product is ours, we'll immediately take the initiative to correct it or work with our customer to improve their application process. If it's from one of our competitors, soon B.I.G. will be scheduling a meeting to demonstrate the superior quality of our offerings – and hopefully land a new customer.

As these stories suggest, when leaders at every level are constantly in touch with the value-added details of the work and the quality challenges they create, the cause of excellence receives a noticeable boost. I like to 'manage by walking around', talking to people at ground level from inside and outside the company, absorbing information, looking for patterns, and sniffing out opportunities. When I am intrigued, puzzled or confused about anything I observe, I ask the magic question, 'Can you tell me exactly *why*?' The answers are always informative – and frequently surprising.

Real leaders take part in the quest for excellence personally, day in and day out. They understand the price of excellence, because they have paid their dues throughout their careers. They resist the temptation to lower the bar at the expense of the whole organization. When extraordinary effort is needed to achieve success, they can put forth that effort and inspire others to do the same – because leaping over the highest bar has become second nature to them.

Is that all there is?

If you think about it, you might be surprised by some of the traits I have not included in this list of six essential leadership qualities.

For example, I have not included intelligence – even though the task of leadership does require careful thought, weighing of evidence, analytical ability, and other activities in which intelligence is advantageous.

But intelligence – sheer brainpower like that exhibited by expert puzzle-solvers, chess masters or mathematics geniuses – is really not essential to great leadership. Most of the successful leaders I know have at least average intelligence; many are above average. And, of course, good judgement is an essential tool of the leader. On the other hand, I know many people who are very, very clever but lack the particular qualities that are required to make them effective leaders. They may be excellent at brain-driven tasks, but it's unlikely they can get others to follow their lead, to work together effectively or to dedicate their energies to an all-important mission. Leadership is not an IQ race.

Another quality whose absence some might find surprising is charisma – the mixture of personal charm, magnetism and grace that inspires excitement and devotion in other people. I describe charisma as 'the fascination of presence'. It is ambiguous to define but easy to recognize, and some of the world's most admired leaders have been gifted with it.

Many people long to be charismatic. The ability to charm others, to make them hang on your every word, may seem highly desirable, but I don't consider charisma a quality that is necessary for leader-ship – nor is it something to strive for. For one thing, consider the fact that many of the world's best leaders are not particularly charismatic. Many are not personally attractive; some appear, at first glance, unimpressive or even boring! The qualities that make them good leaders only become clear over time and through results. Leaders like this may not attract starry-eyed fans, but they do attract stakeholders, especially among people who recognize real leader-ship traits like vision, collaboration, authenticity, commitment to excellence, and the other attributes we've described in this chapter.

Furthermore, charisma can often be found in individuals who are the opposite of good leaders. Some of the world's most infamous tyrants were considered extremely charismatic in their day. Charisma is a natural gift that works as a two-edged sword when it comes to the journey of self-discovery for the leader in you. When used to complement the makings of a true leader in the quest for the six attributes, then charisma can be an ally, but if people draw on their charisma solely in their obsession to be anointed leaders then charisma becomes destructive. That is why, when looking back on history, we see too often how so-called charismatic leaders got the world into trouble!

Thus, charisma can actually be a trap – for leaders and for those around them. Charismatic individuals may find it easy to coast through life rather than embarking on the lifetime journey of self-development. The admiration and acclaim they receive begin to cloud their view. Living an illusion, they stop questioning themselves and hence learn little from experience; they build a wall against those who dare to challenge them; when faced with a tough decision, they wing it, assuming that their 'magic touch' will inevitably lead to triumph. They end up getting themselves and those around them into trouble.

Charisma can also obscure our ability to assess the skills of a would-be leader. Don't make this mistake when judging others. Instead of focusing purely on charisma, look at the six traits we've narrated in this chapter. To measure a potential leader – including yourself – check the six boxes, one by one. They are the true measure of a leader.

The harvest

When you practise the six traits of a leader consistently, day in and day out, the results are visible – not necessarily in extraordinary financial profits, but in the spirit that pervades the organization you belong to. Leadership begins in the heart and mind of a single person, but over time it can shape and uplift an entire organization – and often the larger community as well.

The six qualities I've focused on in this chapter can be found in all leaders. Of course, there are variations in these qualities among different kinds of leaders and in different circumstances. True leaders exhibit these qualities to varying degrees and in varying ways. If you aspire to the ranks of leadership, you need to accept the challenge of developing all six qualities in yourself – every day, with every action you take and every decision you make.

This is the whole meaning of 'the Unknown Leader' and the journey of self-discovery. It begins with a fundamental personal choice – between the low road, the easy path of 'good enough', and the high road of lifetime self-development, or the unflagging quest for excellence. When we choose the high road and stay on it, the feeling is indescribably gratifying. In an ironic way, we feel more natural, more our true selves and more in touch than ever before, as well as experiencing a strong sense of humility. We become better people, better spouses, better parents and better colleagues, and on top of that we possess the fabric and makings of genuine leadership.

Still, the temptations as we embark on this epic journey are not to be underestimated. For starters, we have to fight the natural forces of the status quo, hesitation, or fear of the unknown. Our guide or compass on this journey is our faith in ourselves and in the fact that we are in our present position for a bigger reason and a larger good.

Regardless of the outcome, this journey is a prize in itself, whether we do evolve into the leaders we wish to be or not. Others close to us will see a remarkable difference in how we have developed and evolved. I would say just starting off on this epic journey is a personal triumph in itself, and earns us the designation of 'Unknown Leader in the Making'.

This personal voyage into one's self is a worthy course, though demanding, and requires personal courage and resilience, but let us not allow the mind with its on-and-off tricks to hold us back from experiencing the ride of a lifetime. This journey is our path to discovery or perhaps rediscovery of our new highs. Since this is a lifetime journey, there is no finishing line, no stop signs. We just keep raising the bar at our own pace.

In the end, you'll reach your destination, achieving the heights of leadership without sacrificing quality or compromising your integrity. More importantly, you'll leave behind a legacy that enriches the people you've touched, the organizations you've strengthened and the causes you've championed.

5

Don't hold back! Engaging with the world

In the world of the 21st century, it's not enough simply to be an effective leader within your company, organization or community. It's also necessary to engage with the larger world so that you and the people around you are playing a positive role in making our society richer, fairer and more rewarding for all.

This is a lesson I first began to learn in college, where I pursued a dual major in political science and business, which helped me begin to see the interconnections among all the arenas of human activity. To this day, I like to refer to 'the politics of business and the business of politics' as important connections for every leader to understand.

Engagement in the sense I am describing is about viewing everything you do in a social context. Living in society and giving to society are simply two sides of the same coin, so one of the questions you need to ask yourself about every choice you make, whether in business or in your personal life, is: 'Am I making a positive and lasting difference?' In the long run, this is the most important question we can ask.

Socially responsible business: a modern concept with ancient roots

In the contemporary business world, the idea that our decisions and actions should simultaneously serve both the best interests of our company and the best interests of the community in which we live has drawn increasing attention. In its contemporary form, it goes by various names, including corporate social responsibility (CSR) and sustainability. The latter name emphasizes the concept that sustainable success – that is, long-term success – can only be achieved when the welfare of our world is served by our actions.

Although concepts like CSR and sustainability are now in vogue around the world, they actually have ancient roots in the Middle East. My friend Ghazi Binzagr, who combines the outstanding qualities of a business leader and those of a thoughtful scholar (and whose life and work I recounted in Chapter 1), describes how his upbringing taught him to understand and appreciate the traditional virtues of the business person as conceived in Islamic culture:

> *I come from one of the merchant families in Jeddah, and that is significant to me because there are important values in that merchant culture that underlie our views of leadership. In the old merchant culture, one believed in living for the fulfilment of one's own obligations while simultaneously contributing to one's community. In fact, these two things were seen as one and the same. In terms of our religious value system, we would say we are pursuing our interests in both this world and the hereafter. The idea is that, with each and every stroke, you must fulfil both at the same time. You are not seeking to make profit with one hand while trying to do good with the other. They have to be one and the same.*

In later life, Dr Ghazi found that some of the same ideas are recognized and practised among traditional merchant families outside the region – for example, in Europe. So perhaps, he says, there is a universal 'merchant culture' that values community enrichment not merely in Islam, but around the world.

Of course, business is a competitive arena, and sometimes, in the course of that competition, we divide the world into 'us' and 'them'. The division may be between our company and other companies that are rivals with us for business, or between us and the suppliers we buy from, or between us and the customers we sell to. The distinctions are real and important, but when we let this division of the world into 'us' and 'them' become a division between 'good guys' and 'bad guys', or 'friends' and 'enemies', then we are making a mistake. The world should not be split up into black and white, rival clans. Competition is good – but it's important to compete on the basis of mutual respect, with the goal that everyone, in the end, should benefit in one way or another from the business we transact. We want to strike a good bargain for ourselves – but not to the extent of destroying a rival, exploiting a supplier or cheating a customer.

In today's business arena, this principle of mutual benefit is practised in a wide variety of ways. Being environmentally responsible is one example. A business that produces needless waste, pollutes the air or water, or destroys resources thoughtlessly while pursuing short-term profit is harming the community and violating the spirit of caring engagement with the world. Companies that take their social responsibilities seriously do more than just comply with laws and regulations in regard to the environment – they proactively look for opportunities to enhance and enrich the ecosystems in which they operate, doing whatever they can to make the world a healthier place for all living things.

Practical challenges facing the socially responsible business

I subscribe to the belief that business people have a responsibility to help make the world a better place. I see businesses as having a dual role – serving their shareholders and serving the needs of society. To be judged as truly successful, a company must excel at both.

Balancing these two roles isn't always easy. One of the challenges faced by today's business leaders is developing a strategy and a set of principles that will enable their organizations to achieve both goals consistently. It is fundamental that we must manage our companies so that they compete effectively in the marketplace, attract growing numbers of customers, and produce profits that will benefit share-holders, benefit employees, create jobs, enhance opportunities for learning, and allow investment in even more growth.

If a company goes out of business because of intense competition, changing technology or marketplace shifts – or because the leaders failed to keep their eye on the profit ball – it certainly can't help society. Instead, it will cause suffering on the part of employees, their families, and the suppliers and other organizations that were count-ing on future business dealings with the failed company. Making sure the business you run is on a sound financial footing is the first prerequisite to practising social responsibility.

Once this prerequisite is attained, the corporate culture must recognize the need to engage society in a constructive, positive fashion. But how is this goal to be achieved? There are almost as many good answers as there are successful companies.

Many organizations focus their engagement efforts on environmental stewardship. Others focus on providing educational opportunities through internships, apprenticeships and training programmes, or on supporting economic growth by purchasing from local suppliers, including small businesses. Still others focus on promoting social justice by employing or doing business with groups that are marginalized or disadvantaged. Thoughtful leaders have found ways to carry out these and other activities in such a way as to bring financial rewards to shareholders while also bringing social benefits to everyone in the community.

Along with my board colleagues at B.I.G., I've given a lot of thought to the question of how our company can best serve the needs of society while paying close attention to our bottom line. It seems to me that a business should be able to identify one or more ways of being socially responsible that are a natural outgrowth of the company's purpose – ways that don't feel 'forced', like a hasty or jerry-rigged attempt to impress outsiders or the news media. (This goes back to my emphasis on authenticity as one of the crucial elements of true leadership.) Ideally, practising social responsibility should be second nature to everyone in the company, expressed through actions that capture and embody what is unique and admirable about the organization and its people.

Additional reflection and conversation with philanthropists whose opinions I value have yielded several more key points that I think should guide corporate thinking about CSR.

One worthwhile approach to CSR can be to identify a social need that is not currently being met and that could be addressed through resources your company can provide. Such 'resources' might include money, but they are likely also to include many other kinds of resources, including employee time and talent, unique capabilities, products and services, networks of connections, and so on. Once you've matched up an outside need to the resources you can offer, you can design a programme or initiative to link the two and thereby meet the unmet social need.

In some cases, social needs are already being partially met by existing programmes that need help to scale up, expand their operations or tackle new but closely related issues. When this is the case, a company can positively engage with society by 'adopting' an existing programme and providing it with financial support and other resources. For example, a company that makes health care products could identify a clinic that is already doing a great job of providing services to the poor and then arrange to donate products, and perhaps employee volunteer time, to help the clinic expand its offerings to more locations.

Whatever CSR path a company chooses, it should strive to make sustainable long-term commitments rather than providing stop-and-go funding. It's frustrating for organizations dedicated to social goals when they receive a generous grant from a corporate donor and expand their programmes on that basis, only to find that the moneys have totally dried up a year later.

Company-sponsored CSR programmes should also aim at creating self-supporting social programmes. The ideal would be to help launch a programme headed by a smart, energetic young leader who has a plan to raise funds for the ongoing life of the programme from other community sources. Charity to help the very poor will probably always be necessary, but to the extent possible we should strive to help non-profit organizations escape from dependence on corporate donations for their day-to-day operations.

Finally, I think it's important that company CSR efforts should not become elitist. In my view, being 'socially responsible' should mean helping ordinary people, not providing services to those who are already well off. I would be much more inclined to devote resources to supporting programmes that address needs such as health care, education, housing, nutrition and community development than to give money to organizations devoted to high culture – museums and theatre companies, for example. I have nothing against high culture – on the contrary, I find it exhilarating and elating! But the largely well-off audiences that appreciate such offerings can afford to pay full price for them. Companies that want to help those in need should aim lower on the social ladder.

Guided by these principles, we've decided to focus the CSR projects sponsored by B.I.G. on the theme of enterprise leadership. As this book makes clear, I believe that finding, supporting and encouraging the development of leadership talent at every level of society are crucial to the future of the Middle East. I also recognize that many young people don't have ready access to the educational resources needed to cultivate and enhance their innate leadership abilities. Furthermore, some young people who have made themselves into noteworthy leaders through sheer individual effort have not received the recognition they deserve – and such acknowledgement could in turn encourage other young people to follow in their footsteps. This lack of what you might call 'leadership development infrastructure' is the crucial social gap that B.I.G. endeavours to help remedy.

In Chapters 7, 8 and 9, I'll discuss in more detail some of the specific initiatives B.I.G. is supporting in this area. They include the Ambassadors Program at Effat University in Jeddah, Saudi Arabia, which provides leadership experience and peer-to-peer educational support for promising young women; a unique new mentorship programme at Franklin College in Switzerland, designed to help students from the Middle East and elsewhere make the often difficult adjustment to living far from home for the first time; the chair of Islamic Economics, Finance and Management at Rice University in Texas, which helps to spread awareness of the rich legacy in Islamic culture and literature of wisdom about leadership, management and finance; and the Achievers Award, an annual prize recognizing outstanding young women leaders from Saudi Arabia, including one from the private sector and one from the academic or non-profit world.

Though each of these programmes is different, they all share a common goal – to raise the profile of enterprise leadership as a vital issue among young people from the Middle East. I believe it's a goal that flows naturally from the character and corporate culture of B.I.G., where we strive to be dedicated developers of talented leaders equipped for 21st-century competition.

This is not to say that leadership is the only area in which B.I.G. strives to demonstrate its strong commitment to corporate social responsibility. Our goal is to be among the leading companies in the region in every area of business sustainability. For example, we consider our track record as stewards of the natural environment to be an outstanding one.

We've made some unconventional decisions in pursuit of 'green' performance. For instance, we deliberately resisted the temptation to use plastic materials in our packaging solutions because of the toll that plastics take on the atmosphere and the burden they place on landfills. Instead, our 'naturepak' products are made solely with recyclable fibre-based materials. In effect, if it doesn't grow in a forest, you won't find it in our packages. There's a price to be paid for this kind of environmental commitment, but we are happy to pay it because we share the same planet with our customers – and we share their concern for its future.

We also are proud of our strong employee health and safety programme, and our policy of strict compliance with the highest standards when it comes to working conditions. We consider ourselves fortunate that we've never experienced a work-related casualty in any of our factories, and it has been years since any of our employees suffered a serious injury. Maintaining a record like this is not easy – it takes only one moment of carelessness to cause a tragedy – but we consider it one of our most solemn responsibilities and work at it every day.

One indication of the seriousness with which we take environmental and safety concerns is the fact that we have incorporated measurements of performance in both areas into our LEAP programme. Standing for Leadership, Excellence, Adaptability and Performance, LEAP is the competitive arsenal B.I.G. is using to maintain and expand its leadership among industrial firms in the MENA region. Both a system for developing sound competitive strategy and a tool for tracking divisional and overall corporate achievement, LEAP has helped us steadily upgrade our people and our processes since its creation.

LEAP is a kind of 'road map' for the transformational journey B.I.G. has undertaken – and that includes an unyielding commitment to treat both our own people and the environment with the utmost respect. B.I.G.'s goal is to be ahead of the curve by every meaningful business standard – and that includes social responsibility.

DR HAIFA AL-LAIL
The leader as change agent

As my discussion of CSR suggests, engagement with the world isn't just about avoiding harm – complying with laws and regulations, for example. It's also about working to promote positive social change even as you pursue the highest possible level of personal and organizational success – making the world a better place at the same time as you strive to fulfil your personal ambitions and realize the vision that inspires you.

The point is that companies, non-profit organizations and the individuals who lead them can and should do much more than just maintain the status quo. They can also be change agents, whose work produces benefits that can extend to the entire community, the nation and sometimes even the world.

Dr Haifa Al-Lail has long prided herself on being such a change agent. She is someone who consciously uses her work as a lever for introducing positive improvements into the world around her.

I first met Dr Haifa at a dinner party in honour of the president of the American University of Cairo, where she happened to be sitting at the same table as me. Her sparkling intellect and thoughtful demeanour were immediately apparent. A few months later, when my friend Erik O Nielsen, president of Franklin College, was visiting Jeddah, I took him to see Effat University, the first private university for women in Saudi Arabia, which Dr Haifa serves as president. During the visit, I found out that Dr Haifa had already met Dr Nielsen when she gave a speech in Washington, DC.

Through these encounters, I came to discover Dr Haifa's exceptional commitment both to Effat University and to women's advancement in society. Subsequently, she invited me to address her students, and B.I.G. decided to co-sponsor the university's Ambassadors Program, a scholarship initiative I'll explain more fully in Chapter 8 and that mirrors B.I.G.'s own commitment to leadership development. I also got to know Dr Haifa's husband, Dr Ahmed Gabbani, a strategic human resources executive who is passionate about human capital development, particularly in Jeddah. Together, they are a dynamic couple selflessly devoted to engaging the world and making a positive difference in the lives of countless people.

Today, as president of Effat University, Dr Haifa is serving the young women of Saudi Arabia, providing them with skills, knowledge, insights and attitudes that will enable them to play a dynamic role in building an exciting future for their country and the entire MENA region. However, her role as change agent began in a simple way, when she was working as an assistant professor in the public administration department at King Abdulaziz University. When Dr Haifa joined the department in 1992, one of the first things she noticed was the kind of computer technology available to the professors and students. The university was equipped not with PCs but with mini-computer terminals – a cumbersome, old-fashioned technology that had been outmoded for at least a decade.

'My goodness,' Dr Haifa recalls thinking, 'this is really not going to work!' She responded not by submitting a request to the college administration or raising the issue in a committee meeting, but by simply visiting a local computer store and immediately ordering six PCs and a printer – not just for her department, but for the entire university. 'I couldn't buy everybody a computer,' she says, 'but I wanted just to give them the taste of it.' Since no funds were budgeted for the purchase, she convinced the computer company to donate the devices, telling the manager, 'It's a promotion for you. Once the professors get addicted to PCs, then they will come to buy from you.'

At first, the university administrators weren't pleased with Dr Haifa's bold action. They weren't accustomed to someone creating change simply by *doing* it. But once the faculty and students began using the PCs and marvelling at their speed and flexibility, the administrators changed their minds and began to appreciate Dr Haifa's initiative. After just a year, she was promoted to dean of the girls' section, and soon thereafter she became leader of seven colleges within the university, including the medical college.

There are several valuable lessons for would-be leaders in Dr Haifa's first foray into the role of change agent. When you seek to create change, be sure the change you generate is positive, not disruptive. At first, you may need to take small steps in your drive toward achieving big goals. Starting with modest achievements is fine – there's no reason to feel embarrassed or hesitant about pursuing ideas that seem simple. Above all, don't feel you need to wait until you are in a position of authority or power before trying to bring about positive change. Look for opportunities to make a difference wherever you are right now – and start today.

With her promotion to dean, Dr Haifa was just getting started in her career as a change agent. One thing she quickly realized was that she would need public understanding and support for some of the changes she hoped to introduce to university education – for instance, the expansion of opportunities for young women – so she began writing a regular column for two newspapers, *Okaz* and *Al Madina*. 'I didn't want to rock the boat', she explains. 'I just wanted to introduce ideas and allow people to get to know me and what I stood for. And at that time, writing in the local newspaper was the only way to connect yourself with the community, so I took advantage of the opportunity.'

Not everyone who appears in the media is a real leader, of course. Leadership is about *doing*, not just talking. However, strong leadership does require communication, information and persuasion – the keys to winning hearts, minds and support for your ideas. So Dr Haifa's step of writing regularly for the newspapers – an unusual one for a university administrator – was a smart act of leadership on her part.

Continually improving her communication skills has become a lifelong mission for Dr Haifa. Years later, in the wake of the attacks of 11 September 2001 on the United States, relations between the United States and Saudi Arabia suffered a serious rupture. Many Americans failed to appreciate the fact that the attacks were the work of just a handful of radical terrorists, not representative of the attitudes of Saudi citizens or Muslims in general. To correct these misapprehensions, the Saudi government created outreach programmes to send several distinguished citizens to the United States, to explain Saudi culture, the Saudi political system, and the long-standing friendship between the two nations. These citizen ambassadors visited businesses, colleges, universities, government offices and even military posts in locations throughout the United States.

Dr Haifa was one of the citizens chosen for this programme. While she was a notable public figure by this time, she realized that this new assignment would call forth new leadership qualities in her:

I discovered that representing your country before the world is a unique kind of leadership challenge. If you want to represent your country well, you need to equip yourself in many ways – the way you look, the way you speak, the way you express your beliefs, and how you communicate to others. Public speaking was a new skill for me, so I was shy about it – not because I didn't have self-confidence, but because I'd never really tried it.

Recognizing her limitations as a public spokesperson, Dr Haifa sought training from a professional speaking coach. She watched videotapes of herself discussing cultural topics and responding to questions; she listened to feedback from people who reacted to her speaking style; and she practised specific presentation techniques, such as making eye contact with listeners, controlling her physical gestures to emphasize key ideas rather than distracting the audience, using stories of specific incidents to illustrate themes vividly, and 'speaking from the heart' rather than merely from the mind. Gradually she improved her speaking skills, and today she is a polished and accomplished public advocate for her causes of female power and advancement – an important leadership ability that she developed through a deliberate educational programme in mid-life.

As the first dean at King Abdulaziz University, Dr Haifa was eager to maximize the strengths of the institution for the benefit of students, so she undertook what she calls a SWOT analysis of the university – that is, a careful listing of its strengths, weaknesses, opportunities and threats. She says:

In any new assignment I always try to start with really knowing what is going on around me, so scanning the environment was really an important step – knowing exactly who and what and why, and what is the urgency, and what's the priority? I've found that when you see something that you need to do immediately, and you don't take care of it, the problem will increase, so urgent matters should always be solved immediately if possible.

At King Abdulaziz University, the most urgent need Dr Haifa discovered was the poor condition of housing for female students. She tackled the problem head on, calling the president of the university and saying, 'Look at these buildings. They are in terrible shape. And who is living in them? These are our girls, our daughters. It's really not right to see our daughters living in buildings like these. They need to be demolished.'

This personal appeal, emphasizing the seriousness of the problem through the emotional reference to 'our girls, our daughters' succeeded in capturing the president's attention and winning his support – in theory. But how would she solve the problem in practical terms?

Dr Haifa had an answer. In her SWOT analysis, she observed that the university campus included some vacant buildings that could be converted into student housing. The only problem was that her limited budget was far too small to manage the conversions, so Dr Haifa began putting together a plan to raise the necessary funds.

The plan hinged on soliciting community support, asking wealthy individuals and corporations to donate money. This wasn't easy to do. In the United States, community donations to local colleges and universities are commonplace; the practice is less well established in Saudi Arabia, especially with regard to public institutions like King Abdulaziz University. As a result, Dr Haifa had to invest considerable time, effort and energy into winning converts. (The fact that she had laid the groundwork through her newspaper columns was helpful.)

Over time, she gradually persuaded a number of organizations and individuals to make generous contributions, both in money and in supplies or services, to the student housing project. Within a couple of years, her female students were relocated to newly renovated apartments befitting members of a great university community.

Practically every leader encounters problems that can't be solved through the obvious, ordinary solutions. At times like this, creative thinking is essential. The modest university budget Dr Haifa controlled directly was not enough to pay for the housing conversions her students desperately needed, so Dr Haifa, in her role as leader and change agent, invented a new way of raising funds and did what she had to do to make it work.

Later, when a new college for women in Jeddah was being planned, it was natural that Dr Haifa became part of the team that was offering ideas for how to structure and organize its programme. After all, she had already established herself as a change leader in the field of women's education through her work at King Abdulaziz University. When Dr Haifa was asked to served as president of the new Effat University, it gave her the opportunity to implement some even more ambitious ideas about how to expand and improve opportunities for women in Saudi Arabia.

Having studied in the United States, Dr Haifa was familiar with the Western concept of a 'liberal arts education' – a university curriculum built around a wide array of courses in fields such as history, literature, philosophy, the arts and the sciences, with students being given relative freedom to choose among all these offerings, tailoring a programme to meet their individual interests and needs. By contrast, the traditional curriculum in Saudi Arabia at the time was more rigidly structured, with a series of core requirements that usually include several courses of Islamic study, two courses of Arabic, and three or four courses in either geography or history and communication. Training in critical thinking was de-emphasized, and so was interdisciplinary study that allows students to cross topical boundaries to pursue themes or problems of special concern.

Having experienced it personally during her years of study in the West, Dr Haifa was a believer in the value of the liberal arts programme, and she was eager to introduce it to Effat University. However, she understood the attachment many people feel to the traditional curriculum, including, of course, influential individuals in the Ministry of Education. She carefully tailored her curriculum proposals to make them adaptable to Saudi culture. Rather than using the term 'liberal arts', which is unfamiliar to most Saudis, she called her plan a 'general education programme', which received an almost universally positive response. Dr Haifa observes:

This kind of equation makes a big difference in leadership. You always need to think about the balance that you're trying to strike between the outside world and its culture and the system you are trying to create. If you want really to lead, you always need to seek a fair balance between the different demands that groups and individuals bring to the table.

For Effat University, the balance Dr Haifa describes is between tradition and modernity, between Western approaches and Muslim ones, between secular and faith-based philosophies. Dr Haifa says:

Effat University is proud to be Saudi, but that doesn't prevent us from acquiring the best of what the world offers. That's why we have relationships with universities and colleges all over the world, in Japan, China, America, Europe. We bring in lecturers and teachers with an international perspective who can enrich what our students are learning and help them understand our national and regional culture in a global context.

At the same time, Effat University and Dr Haifa continue to push aside barriers that limit what young students – particularly Saudi women – can achieve. She says:

We pride ourselves on offering subjects that are unique. For example, engineering was never previously offered as a course of study to females in the Kingdom, so our engineering programme represents a great example of what Effat is all about. The same is true of other fields of study, such as architecture. Last year we graduated our first class in electrical computer engineering – three students, two of whom are now working in mobile communications here in Saudi Arabia, while the third has gone on to pursue a PhD in the field. And then there is our master's degree programme in Islamic finance, a field that has never been offered in any other university, whether male, female or co-ed. Effat is breaking new ground in all these areas.

It takes a special kind of leader to guide an organization successfully through the winds of change. Dr Haifa Al-Lail is one such leader. Thanks to her pioneering spirit, her deep understanding of human motivation, her strong communication skills and her profound determination to make a difference, she is changing the face of Saudi education for thousands of young women, opening doors that otherwise might still remain shut.

Keeping pace with the world: a marathon, not a sprint

Once you commit yourself to achieving social goals alongside personal, career or business objectives, you may find yourself experiencing times of impatience and frustration. After all, social change on a significant scale – such as the positive change in business practices in the Middle East that B.I.G. is actively engaged in delivering – is a very slow process, with both setbacks and triumphs. It's important not to let this sense of impatience derail your efforts or tempt you to become discouraged. Think about how a small stream of water, flowing persistently over time, can carve an entire landscape. If you pursue your objectives consistently and leave behind an organization – or even just a handful of people – whose lives you've influenced, eventually your work, like that stream of water, may produce changes you can't foresee.

A colleague of mine has thought a lot about the social issues related to gender discrimination and the frustrations that are sometimes involved, for her and others, in trying to overcome it:

I think the only way to get over the feeling that life is unfair is to think about what you can do to be part of something that changes that. For example, when I joined my first organization, I got an offer from them, and I negotiated for higher compensation, and I got what I negotiated for, and after joining I learned that, in fact, there were many people there who had much lower qualifications than me who had received higher compensation, and had continued to receive promotions.

This kind of salary gap is a worldwide phenomenon, but rather than being really upset about that, I kind of felt, OK, I'm going to be now in a position where I have to hire people. I want to make sure that this doesn't happen to them, because, if it does, then I'm perpetuating the same problem. The people that I hire need to be paid equivalent to somebody else, not based on something like their gender or whatever. It needs to really be based on something.

So don't focus on the frustration you may feel over not finishing what you set out to do during your lifetime and on your watch. Focus on the positive changes you can make, and think long-term, not short-term. Above all, remember that the notion of social responsibility applies not just to the organizations for which we work, but to each of us individually. You and I have a personal responsibility to make the world a better place – especially the corner of it where we live, and the people whose lives we touch.

That is why, in the end, I define my own approach to leadership through the concept of 'servant leadership'. My job as leader is to serve those who serve my organization – to enhance their lives, appreciate and reward their good work, and create an environment in which their talents and creativity can thrive. It's one of the ultimate social responsibilities that every leader needs to shoulder – because if we don't do it, than who will?

6

Faith: the shelter
of the mind

In the hubbub of daily existence, we busy ourselves by filling our 'life suitcases' with everything we need for our lifetime journey: educational credentials, work experiences, personal contacts, impressive achievements. These things are very important, but equally important is that *other* suitcase, standing in the corner, which we will take on the ultimate journey into the next life. Most of us assume that journey is far in the future and that we will have plenty of time to pack for our departure. This of course may be an illusion, since no one can foretell the future – and in any case the years have a way of passing much more quickly than we anticipate.

It's never too early to begin thinking about that journey and the gear we'll need. Have you been thinking about the suitcase in the corner? Have you begun filling it with the personal and spiritual attributes you'll want when the next great phase of life begins?

Mindful of these questions, I've found that a consistent sense of faith has been increasingly important to me as a corporate leader. However, it's important to understand what this means. Faith is not necessarily the same as religion, nor is it to be identified with any particular religion. Faith is about nourishing your connection with the greater power, whether you call this power Allah, God or simply the Creator that sustains us all. Faith in this sense should lead one to greater openness, a deeper appreciation for other people, and a richer sense of joy in life – not negativity, guilt, fear or a desire to judge and condemn others.

I try to practise my own faith in a way that feels natural. For me, that means braiding prayer, reflection, study and meditation into my everyday life as a business person, a husband and father, a friend and an engaged citizen. Practicing my faith is not just about withdrawing from the world and seeking purity through solitude. And it's not just about being obvious and overt about my religious practices and beliefs, or trying to persuade others to share them. My faith is something far deeper and very personal, based on my own relationship with my Creator, and the same goes for you; it is a unique bond, like no other.

Although each of us has a faith and a one-of-a-kind connection to God, we can learn from one another. Through self-examination and through probing conversations with friends, colleagues and people I admire, I've come to learn that faith plays many important roles in the lives of those who are blessed with it.

Faith as a moral lighthouse

One role of faith is to be our ethical guidepost. The teachings of the divine religions vary, but all are remarkably consistent in the moral principles they offer for dealing with our fellow human beings. All exalt such central values as honesty, altruism, compassion, generosity, mercy, forgiveness, tolerance and love. And all caution us against pursuing earthly benefits – riches, power, fame, pride – at the expense of the welfare of other people. Those people who immerse themselves in the teachings of religion – whether they study the divine books or the wisdom of any of the world's great prophets – will find themselves continually reminded of the need to treat others with justice and kindness, despite the many opportunities and temptations to do the opposite that surround us in the worlds of business and practical affairs.

The argument that there is a deep-rooted link between being religious and being a person of honour has been established over centuries. There's no question that faith in a supreme being has been a powerful support to millions of people when they are struggling to obey the dictates of conscience.

Even more powerful on this score are the teachings of the Prophet Muhammed (Peace Be Upon Him) himself. We learn from him that pursuit of perfection, in all its forms, is the mission of all humans, and the result is love of God. Thus it is faith that gives us the guidance and the will-power to strive constantly to become better men and women – and it is faith that ultimately rewards us when we reach the end of our life's journey and beyond.

Faith as a source of stamina

There will be times in life when difficult experiences make you want to throw in the towel. Faith plays a crucial role when we are dealing with such adversity; it serves as an anchor in times when despair is a strong temptation. It also serves as a compass in times of success, when it's easy to lose sight of reality and become puffed up with conceit. Since faith becomes important in various ways at different times – often unexpectedly – the wise leader pays attention to deepening his or her faith from an early age, so this essential support is available when the need arises.

In Islam, we pray facing Mecca five times a day – a unique religious practice that is also a powerful mental and spiritual discipline that does for the mind and the heart what exercise does for the body: keeps it sound and strong for the tests of life. Just as a habit of daily exercise quickly becomes second nature, so does the habit of communing with God. In time, it comes effortlessly. In fact, just as the body begins to ask for exercise once the habit is established, the soul begins asking for prayer – a very healthy craving.

The benefits of daily prayer go beyond the spiritual discipline it provides. Leaving the world behind for a few minutes at a time also helps put the issues of daily life into a broader perspective – and often has helped me to think more clearly about business and personal challenges and see them from several angles.

I once knew someone with great strength of character who subscribed to the myth that he was 'in control' of his life. When adversity struck, he suddenly faced the possibility of losing control, which he found deeply troubling. I told my friend:

> *Listening to what I'm going to say may take you aback,*
> *but the truth is that you are really not in control. When*
> *you make faith the centre of your actions, you will realize*
> *that there is something called destiny that determines our*
> *fate, regardless of our efforts to do the very best that we*
> *are capable of. We are not in control of what happens to us.*
> *We are only in control to the extent of our faith – faith in*
> *what we believe in and faith in ourselves. Beyond that, the*
> *feeling of being in control is simply an illusion.*

Here's an example I think everyone can identify with. Take a moment to think about the people who have had the greatest influence in your life – loved ones, close friends, mentors, teachers, advisers, colleagues. Then think about how you happened to meet each of these people. Was it the result of a deliberate plan on your part? Or was it, in fact, due to happenstance, coincidence and chance? For most of us, the best things we experience come about through fortunate accidents far more often than planning. Reflecting on this fact makes us quickly realize how little control we really have over the bigger picture in our lives.

So the more control we have over things in our lives, the more we realize how little control we actually have. It's a paradox worthy of further exploration.

Meanwhile, we need to nourish faith on a daily basis. It's the source of inner strength we must rely on when times get tough. Think about the tyre on your car: If it's not inflated properly, it will get damaged the first time you drive over a pothole or a bit of broken glass, but when the air pressure *inside* your tyre is just right, the tyre will be able to withstand pressure from *outside*.

Faith works in a similar way: Inner strength gives us the outer strength we need to survive the risks on life's many highways and byways. When you rely on faith to help you learn how to manage the pressures of life and work, you'll find those pressures can become a source of inspiration and motivation. Stress can turn into bliss. Look to faith to help you get there.

Faith can help us avoid the excessive pride in oneself that we call conceit, arrogance or hubris. It reminds us how little in life we completely control, and how much we must rely on a power greater than ourselves in times of adversity.

Faith, properly understood, can also strengthen our belief in ourselves. If we don't believe in ourselves and our mission in life, chances are that no one else will believe in us. While recognizing our limits, we can develop a deeper sense of faith in our skills, our abilities, our judgements, our heritage and the values we've inherited from our families and our communities. After all, the Creator conceived, formed and placed us on this earth to serve a purpose – to do good, to enrich those around us, to help fulfil the Creator's will. And since he is all-knowing, he would not have designed us to be inadequate to the task before each one of us.

Therefore we must accept the truth that God has created and shaped us with the capabilities needed to perform the jobs he has set before us. Recognizing this reality gives us the strength to push forward when the path ahead is particularly steep and rocky. We need to have faith in the fact that our Creator has well fitted us for the journey, and the trials for which he has prepared us make that journey especially worthwhile. Those trials test our faith – but they also develop it and, ultimately, confirm it. The taller the mountain, the greater the test – and the stronger the faith we enjoy when we finally reach the summit.

As we've noted, the journey of leadership is like an expedition to Everest. Failures and successes, criticism and praise, setbacks and advances – in a lifetime, we'll experience them all. The enduring spirit that keeps us going is faith.

The bigger picture

Faith in oneself and in the attributes God has given you is essential, but we also need faith in something larger than ourselves. Whatever talents we may have, and no matter what role in life we've been asked to fill, each of us is only one person in a very big universe – a universe whose destiny is unfolding over billions of years in accordance with a plan that none of us can completely absorb.

Recognizing how small we are in comparison to the grand vision of the Creator is humbling. It can be daunting, making us question whether we have the strength to fulfil our part in the plans that God has made. However, in the end it is comforting. When I feel discouraged about my limitations, about my weaknesses, about mistakes I have made or failures I've experienced, it is a relief to reflect that I am just one small piece in a giant puzzle whose shape I can glimpse only dimly. The Creator who has designed it all is capable of using me, and all of us – with all our inadequacies – to bring his plan to fruition.

At the end of the day, all we can do is strive to the utmost to fulfil our roles to the very best of our abilities. Everything beyond that is up to a power far greater and wiser than all of us – and remembering that makes it easier for me to sleep soundly at night.

Faith and the pursuit of the obvious

I've said that faith and religion are not identical. Can a person who experiences flashes of doubt about faith or religion be considered a person of faith?

Let's begin with the question of doubt. Doubt as a matter of searching is not a sin. Rather, it is a natural part of the human condition. We live in a complicated world in which good and evil, truth and falsehood, order and chaos are constantly intermingled and for some people frequently blurred. In such a world, it's inevitable that we should experience times of doubt. Such moments are often the launching pad for deeper reflection on the meaning of life, the realities of existence, and our ultimate purpose. Many of the wisest spiritual teachers and scholars from every culture achieved that status by passing through a period of intense doubt, which led them in the end to a more profound understanding of the world – and of their Creator.

No wonder God is so compassionate and patient with us when we experience doubt. Doubt is often the first step on a long journey that leads, ultimately, into his mercy.

If you find yourself experiencing doubt about your faith, don't let this become a state of mind; keep contemplating and searching for answers. Doubt can be a stepping stone toward enlightenment – provided it is a humble doubt, which recognizes the world's vastness, its richness of meaning, and our own minuscule size by comparison. Contemplation of this world, though it may begin in doubt, often ends in the discovery of the Creator's will behind it all.

A period of doubt can also be a trigger for self-education. All of the world's great religious traditions have left behind rich texts of wisdom and advice that have shaped and expanded the consciousness of millions of men and women. Study some of the great texts; seek guidance as to their deeper meaning from scholars, teachers and spiritual philosophers; reflect on how the words of the sages relate to the challenges of your own life. You may never resolve all of your doubts, but the chances are good that you will gain insights of profound value to you as you continue your lifetime journey.

In the end, we are all, in one way or another, people of faith – because the only alternative is a life without meaning. So when it comes to religion and issues of faith, tread carefully. Then the obvious will fall into our grasp.

Whatever your personal beliefs, your journey as a leader will be immeasurably enhanced if you work on developing your faith just as you develop your other forms of skill, knowledge and self-discipline. With faith as your constant companion, you will learn more, understand more, accomplish greater things, and experience the ups and downs of your journey more fully and deeply. This is a choice you should make early in your life.

Our life here on earth is a time for planting seeds and for watering the soil. Ultimately there will be a time for harvest, whether here on earth or in the life to come. But the quality of the seeds you plant and the diligence and care with which you tend the sprouts as they grow will come back some day to determine the quality of the harvest you'll receive.

Part Two

Developing
leadership in motion

7

The making of
a global leader

The world of the 21st century is a uniquely challenging environment, not just for business leaders but for anyone who aspires to leadership in any context. As we've discussed, the traditional model of top-down, autocratic leadership, symbolized by the general on his horse ordering soldiers into battle, is increasingly obsolete in a world that is global, culturally diverse, technologically complex and rapidly changing – a world where collaboration among people of widely differing skills is essential to success. Those of us who are in the Middle East are called upon to adapt our views of leadership to accommodate these new realities.

In this chapter, I'll present some ideas about what we must consider to remain competitive and create a lasting foundation of prosperity for this new era. Much of the advice I'll offer is directed at individual readers in the midst of their lifetime journeys of self-discovery. I'll start with a bit of a warning: Don't assume that, because you plan to remain in the MENA region, the influences and demands of global business won't apply to you. The competition for leadership is no longer merely national or even regional – it is global.

I hope that young people eager to prepare themselves to build great careers in the 21st century will benefit from my observations about the new global environment and the skills they'll need to engage in it effectively. I also hope that others interested in the leadership challenges faced by the region (and indeed by countries around the world) will find much of interest in these pages. I'll suggest some important ways that all of us in both the private and public sectors can work together to help create opportunities for the spirit of global leadership to thrive among our youth.

The familiar African proverb says 'It takes a village to raise a child'. I might apply the same philosophy to the theme of this chapter, with a bit of a twist: 'It takes a society to create a global leader.'

Learning from the world – one man's journey

To prepare the region for this new era of global competition, one psychological and social change we need to make is to foster a spirit of greater inclusiveness for all kinds of people. As leaders, we need to break down traditional biases concerning geographic, ethnic and other differences, and be prepared to recognize, support and reward talent wherever it flourishes.

We also need an increased willingness to reach out to the world beyond the borders of the region and the Muslim faith. Here, my own experiences as a student and later as a senior corporate executive in making connections with people from Europe and North America have been especially instructive.

My father recognized early on the importance of an international education, so the decision was made by my parents that I would leave my home in Jeddah, Saudi Arabia before I was even 10 to go to Lebanon and pursue my education there. This turned into a defining experience for me – partly because of the stimulation I received from living abroad, but even more from attending an innovative US high school programme in Beirut. There was an Arabic component to the programme, and we interacted with very good teachers on the Arabic side, but a handful of the American teachers I studied under during my teen years in Lebanon pushed me and my fellow students to interact with them personally and even to question what they were saying in a way that is more characteristic of US education than the more traditional, conservative schooling experienced in the Middle East at that time.

I remember one teacher in particular, I believe from the state of Kentucky, who taught a class in world history and a business course. His name was Mr Taylor, and he certainly looked like no teacher I had ever seen. He wore blue jeans and brightly coloured, patterned shirts, and had long hair that made him appear like what we then called a hippie. (This was back in the late 1960s.)

Mr Taylor's behaviour in the classroom was equally unconventional. Rather than simply lecture about his subject and expect us to regurgitate the information and ideas he taught us, he would present a narrative about some event from history and then say something like 'Looking back, here's my view of what that public figure did wrong. But what do *you* think?' When all of us in the class said we agreed with him, he wasn't pleased – in fact, he didn't like that at all. Instead, he pushed us to develop our own perspectives and then to defend those views with evidence and arguments. In this way, Mr Taylor developed in us the ability to think for ourselves and to hold our own in debate.

It took some time to get used to this new approach to learning. We students were accustomed to regarding teachers as absolute authorities. If you had doubts or questions about something you heard in class, you wouldn't dream of challenging the teacher in the presence of other students. At most, you might ask him about it, quietly and a bit timidly, afterwards. So at first we were intimidated by our 'hippie teacher' and his challenging style, thinking he might be setting a trap: 'Maybe if we disagree with him', we thought, 'he'll end up failing us in the course.' But when Mr Taylor actually *refused* to let us accept his positions without developing our own good reasons for them, we realized that he was sincere.

I learned a lot from Mr Taylor's class. It taught me not to fear authority, but to recognize it as a source of information and ideas that can be valuable, so long as you don't accept them unthinkingly. I also learned to distinguish between personal animosity and reasoned discussion. The way to learn and grow is to engage in a debate, which is not about disliking or attacking your opponent but about challenging the other person's ideas and testing your own against them. I learned to engage by saying, 'Leaving personality aside, I have an issue with that policy, and these are the reasons.' To begin to develop this approach to learning at the age of 12 or 13 is not common – and it is enormously valuable.

To this day, I'm a great believer in the value of debate and dialogue as a technique for uncovering the truth. When my business colleagues and I are trying to solve a management dilemma or devise a new strategy, I find that open discussion produces the best outcomes, leading to deeper insights and more complete concepts than any single person could hope to develop. Similarly, when I'm asked to visit a university to meet with students, I like to say, 'Let's start with debates', because debates allow students to become engaged in the quest for truth. This, to me, is what education is about: we provide students with knowledge and ideas, and they learn to use those resources to forge new, creative understandings and approaches through the power of engagement and debate.

While I studied in Lebanon, I spent a couple of my summers in England, improving my knowledge of the language – a skill that has proven essential for me on the international business stage. I attended an English programme in a charming little village about an hour north of London known as Sawbridgeworth, famous today because the celebrated English soccer player David Beckham owns a country home there, dubbed 'Beckingham Palace' by the British media. My fellow students in the English classes included a group of lovely young women who were honing their secretarial skills. They used to make a fuss over me – the fact that I was from an exotic part of the world that they associated with *The Arabian Nights* made me in their eyes a charming youngster – and they even competed for the chance to practise their typing skills by typing up the poetry I had an early gift for writing.

The unexpected lesson: you never know what kinds of unexpected experiences will help you develop your social skills and your self-confidence! If I had limited my social life purely to the classroom I might never have gotten over my typical 13-year-old timidity.

From Lebanon, I moved on to an international school in Switzerland, driven in large part by the on-again, off-again civil war that was making life in Beirut very disruptive, at times precarious. In Switzerland, I learned some additional lessons made possible by that unique environment.

For one thing, I developed a special level of comfort in dealing with all kinds of people from many walks of life. My fellow students in Lebanon were all young Arabs like myself, but in Switzerland I encountered students from around the world – Americans, Europeans and a few Asians – and the staff were equally diverse. Some of my classmates came from well-to-do families, while others were middle-class, and some had even been political asylum seekers, forced to flee their homes by social unrest. It was really interesting for me to encounter the broader world for the first time in this open yet protective environment.

In Switzerland, I also began to develop the real hunger for ever-expanding knowledge that has characterized me ever since. I quickly discovered that many of my fellow students, especially the Europeans, had deeper and broader academic backgrounds than mine. They had already been steeped in the basic sources of Western civilization – history, literature, philosophy, the arts and science. I decided I wanted to catch up with my classmates, so I began studying those subjects seriously for the first time, determined to become a man of the world with the kind of global breadth of understanding that the Europeans seemed to enjoy.

This attitude served me well when I moved on to the next phase of my education, when I attended a university in the United States. The institution I chose was not one of the world-renowned US universities in New York, Massachusetts or California, but rather the relatively obscure Rollins College in Winter Park, Florida. (Winter Park is a suburb of Orlando, which at the time was just beginning the process of growing from a sleepy community centred on the citrus-growing business into the major tourist hub it has since become, thanks mainly to the advent of Disney World.)

I had three criteria in mind when I chose Rollins. First, having spent the previous years in Switzerland, I preferred to be in a southern climate (I had had enough of shovelling snow in Switzerland!). Second, I wanted to attend a small, high-quality institution – not one of the giant universities with 50,000 or more students scattered across the United States – and Rollins fitted the bill, having been highly recommended by a friend of my father's who worked at a *Fortune 500* company in Ohio. Finally – and perhaps the most unique requirement – I wanted a place where no Arab students had preceded me and where there were no fellow Arabs to lean upon or to evoke stereotypes, positive or negative. This was not because I was self-conscious of my Arab identity or wanted to assimilate invisibly into Western culture. It's because I wanted to learn about the West in an unfiltered way. My vision was to pioneer a positive image and connection to the West among people who knew little about the Middle East. I hope I did a fair job, although that's something for my successors from the Arab world at Rollins to decide.

At Rollins, I opted to take a dual major programme, studying both political science and business administration. I was thinking about public service at the time, and I had become fascinated by the ways in which personalities shape the future – how individuals can have an impact on world events. That led me to political science.

It was in answer to a question from a Rollins adviser about why I wanted to pursue this dual major that I first spoke the expression I use to this day. 'I'm fascinated by the politics of business and the business of politics', I replied. At one point, I seriously considered attending the Fletcher School of Diplomacy at Tufts University in Massachusetts, but as I examined the realities of public service and the constraints it inevitably involved I realized that I aspired for broader growth opportunities and a faster pace than a government job would allow. And when my father's health began to decline and he said, 'I want to start to take life a little easier', the decision to concentrate on business and, in particular, on the future of our family company became an obvious one. However, the two-sided connection between politics and business continues to intrigue me, and the deeper understanding of human motivations that political science gave me has helped me greatly in my business career.

The courses I took in political science also allowed me to learn to really enjoy reading – not by choice, but by force. I'll always remember my first week in class with Professor Thomas Lairson, who later became my adviser and mentor. He handed us a 400-page book on political theory and said, 'Read this. You'll be expected to answer questions about it in two weeks.' For me this was an unheard-of challenge. Fortunately, Rollins offered a brief course in speed reading that I took along with a lot of other students. It helped me develop the ability to absorb a lot of information quickly, which of course I use every day in my work.

Yet once again the lessons I learned outside the classroom were among the most meaningful. I didn't particularly like the idea of living in a dorm room on the campus, because I felt this would limit my exposure to the United States I was eager to learn more about, so I searched the local community for an alternative. In a few days, I found an apartment near the campus that I thought would make a fine home for my college years. It was owned by an older gentle-man named Joe Jackson, who offered me a proposition. 'You can rent the apartment for $500 per month', Joe said, 'or buy it outright for $55,000.'

I did some calculations, and then approached my father with a proposition of my own. 'If you rent the apartment for me', I said, 'it will cost $24,000 in rent for my contemplated four years in college. But if you buy it, we'll save the rent money, and after I graduate I can resell the apartment to someone else.'

'Do you think you'll be able to sell it for the same amount we have to pay?' my father asked.

Since property in Florida was rising in value at the time, I said I thought so. And I went further. 'If you buy the apartment', I said, 'I'll guarantee the $55,000 resale price – provided you agree to let me keep the difference if I make a profit on the sale.' My father agreed, we bought the apartment, and it made me a cosy home for my years in Florida.

If you are wondering, it turned out that property in the Orlando area rose in value even more quickly than I anticipated. I was able to sell the apartment for a handsome premium. The windfall was large enough that I felt bad about keeping it all, so instead I split the profit, 50/50, with my father.

More important than the profit on our investment, living off-campus made it easy for me to develop a close-knit circle of local friends who included people from beyond the contained milieu of college life. Joe Jackson and his wife Jane turned out to be sweet, kindly neighbours. Colonel Jackson, as many people called him, was full of stories about his experiences in 'the war' (he meant the Second World War, of course). Joe and I became not just neighbours but friends, and over time I got to know several other wonderful local people, including Jim Stroker, who'd been elected the youngest local judge ever at the age of 28, Renzo Bontempo, who worked for Martin Marietta, and Chas Schmidt, who became my dentist – in fact, to this day, when he and his wife Nancy visit us in Europe, Chas still insists on giving my teeth a quick inspection. These are just a few of the Americans I met during my college years who became lifelong friends of mine.

One of my closest American friends was an astute lawyer named Ted Herzog, who became a business associate and adviser. While I was studying in Florida, my father started getting me involved in a number of business arrangements in the United States, serving as the spokesperson in making connections between our company base in Jeddah and the US companies we were doing business with. Ted helped me a lot. He was a door-opener, a detail-oriented evaluator of contracts and agreements, and a skilled communicator from whom I learned a great deal about the arts of negotiation and compromise – particularly in a US context.

Ted also became a hunting companion. (I'd become interested in hunting in a small way back in Lebanon.) Most weekends, when we weren't out having dinner with friends, Ted and I were usually hunting, going after deer, quail, doves or other game, depending on the season, or fishing for largemouth bass or the other great game fish that fill the waters of Florida. I've maintained my interest in hunting to this day. I've enjoyed fine outings in Europe and Africa, but especially in the United States – elk in New Mexico, pheasants in Nebraska, quail in Georgia, trout in California, salmon and caribou in Alaska – all while living a simple outdoor life with few amenities or modern conveniences but plenty of fresh air and good companionship. Hunting has taken me all over the world and enabled me to make many kinds of friends I might never have known otherwise.

I ended up enjoying Rollins so much, both academically and personally, that I chose to stay there for my graduate work, earning an MBA from Rollins in 1980.

A fresh cultural perspective

The years I spent studying in Florida and getting to know Americans on a one-to-one basis taught me a number of valuable lessons about qualities in Western culture – especially in the United States – that I consider noteworthy.

Those qualities include a sense of openness to people of all kinds, a profound appreciation for the value of hard work, and that same readiness to debate almost any issue – to hear all sides of a complicated topic and learn from every perspective – that I had first encountered from American teachers back in Beirut. These traits, which I now share to a large degree, have been very useful to me in business, and I would like to see others from the Middle East be exposed to them.

Americans, I found, are gifted with the ability to give people a first chance. If you're a neighbour in a typical US community – even a new neighbour from an unfamiliar background, as I certainly was when I moved to Winter Park – the chances are good that you'll get a knock on the door and a friendly 'Howdy, neighbour! Is there anything we can do to help you feel at home?' And in situations where there is some kind of controversy to be decided, most Americans extend the same open-minded attitude to the world of ideas. The common attitude you encounter is 'Before we pass judgement, let's listen to what's being said and decide for ourselves what we think.' I consider this a wise and effective approach to the world, whether in business or in other aspects of life.

Another person I befriended in Winter Park was Lowell Watkins, whom everybody called Lou. I went into Lou's store one day to buy some hunting gear, and soon we hit it off and started going on hunting and fishing trips together. Listen to Lou, and you might think he was a stereotypical Southerner like the ones you see on TV or in the movies; he spoke with a drawl, usually moved slowly, and was a simple man. You might jump to the conclusion that Lou didn't have much to offer intellectually, but that would be a mistake. If you listened hard enough, you soon discovered a lot of wisdom underneath Lou's country exterior. The fact that we became friends is even more surprising when you consider that I was in my early 20s at the time, while Lou was over 60, but that's the kind of thing that can happen in an open society like the United States.

I'm not the only person from the Middle East to make a similar discovery about people while visiting the United States. A distinguished businessman I know told me this story about his own experience as a student abroad:

> *One thing I learned while studying in the United States is how people are similar. Sometimes we stereotype people based on their religions, based on their ethnic background and all that, and when you go to a culture that is completely different from your own and you create friendships, you realize that people in the end are people, and their aspirations are similar.*
>
> *Here is an example from my own experience. Growing up with the Palestinian issue and other controversies, you get an image of Judaism and Jewish people that is not usually positive. But when I went to America, the academic adviser assigned to me by my college happened to be Jewish. Not only did he prove to be a fine teacher and an excellent adviser, but we actually became close friends, with a relationship that went beyond a student–teacher relationship. It was an amazing experience, and it helped me discover the value of keeping an open mind about all people until you get to know them as individuals. I learned to never pre-judge.*

As individuals, Americans benefit from their culture of open-mindedness. They develop friendships that might be impossible if they were quick to judge people by their appearance, family background, ethnic history or religion. But the United States also benefits as a society. Contributions by men and women from every corner of the world have helped to build the United States, and today they are helping to keep US companies competitive in a global economy.

What could be more American than those iconic soft drinks Coke and Pepsi? But today the CEO of the Coca-Cola Company is Muhtar Kent, a Muslim man born in New York City to a Turkish father, while the CEO of PepsiCo is Indra Nooyi, a Hindu woman born in Chennai, India. And of course, in 2008, Americans elected a self-described 'skinny kid with a funny name' as their president – Barack Obama, whose father was a scholarship student from Kenya and who spent several of his formative years living with his mother and stepfather in Indonesia.

If you have talent and personality, Americans will accept you, even embrace you, no matter what your background may be. It's a quality I admire, and one that gives their country a competitive edge on the world stage. Americans should never let events – even tragic and painful ones like 9/11 – weaken their commitment to this important value of openness and inclusiveness, which gives them a unique national advantage over others.

Americans also are great believers in – and practitioners of – hard work. During my years in the United States, I saw people at every social level working really hard to make ends meet, to better themselves and to improve their skills: students working in part-time jobs to help pay for their studies; men and women holding down second jobs; and entrepreneurs working nights and weekends to get their struggling young companies off the ground. I got bitten by the same bug, and now I think I set an example of diligence and application for colleagues and younger people at work.

Not much that is truly worthwhile can be accomplished without plenty of hard work; developing a taste for it is one of the best things you can do for yourself when you're young.

Of course, the United States isn't the only place that is blessed by hard-working people. Hard work has always been the hallmarks of earlier generations in the Middle East. But there can also be a tendency on the part of some young people to be a bit complacent, to lack the instinctive drive to work hard.

My friend Nabil Alyousuf, whose story I recounted in Chapter 2, has also noticed this cultural difference, and he suggests two possible reasons for it:

> *One factor is the oil and the sudden wealth it brought to our region. Our fathers were very hard-working, but then our generation, born in the 1960s, or even the generation after us, got complacent. The second factor related to our culture. We tend to be protective, or we embrace family members here, and while that's good it can generate a complacency at the same time. You feel that you always have that safety net; you'll be taken care of by your parents, your family, your extended family and all that. In the US, people tend to be individualistic. They often move far away from their families for work opportunities. The breaking up of families is not a good thing – but the sense of self-reliance encourages hard work. That's one reason why an appreciation for hard work seems to be widespread in America.*

Nabil Alyousuf goes on to point out that this is what is meant by 'the American dream' – the assumption that, if you work hard and take some risks, you can achieve almost anything. It's a dream that can be shared by people from any background – including by those who don't have the opportunity to study abroad.

As you can see, I learned a lot from other cultures during my years of education – in Lebanon, in Switzerland and especially in the United States.

Nurturing cross-cultural learning

In the years that followed, I made more friends among the business community in the United States. Burnell Roberts was chairman and CEO of the Mead Corporation. My father had known and done business with Mead for many years, and I would visit and interpret for him when he visited Jim McSweeney, who was chairman and CEO with Burnell as his second in command. When Jim McSweeney retired, Burnell assumed the leadership role, and we continued the association. I learned a lot from him – his demeanour, his steady hand – and found him a first-class executive. I was fortunate, young as I was, to have the opportunity to learn so much from a business-man of his stature.

There were two or three other Americans I got to know well, par-ticularly in the paper and forest products industry, which was a big component of our work in that country. Dean Stout was a real Irish gentleman as well as a paper guy through and through, who knew that industry like the palm of his hand. Dean reported to Jess Belser, who was president of Continental Forest Industries. Dean was a premier networker – he knew everyone in the industry and opened many a door for me. When I asked for Dean's help to arrange a senior-level contact for me, he would take time to think about it and then call me back, using his favourite line, 'so-and-so is worth a lunch'. He was also a wonderful dinner companion. Story after story would roll out, many of them with some kind of kernel of wisdom at the end to take home. And then there was Jud Hannigan, a big guy, a one-time professional American football player and a former president of International Paper. As Jess Belser's top operations guru, Jud was known to be able to diagnose the condition of a paper mill just by listening to the sound of it running. Good people. I learned a lot from all of them, doing business, making deals, and combining the work schedule with a strong social connection – lunch, dinner, a fishing trip. This is how bonds are created, trust is built, and relationships are established that can last for years.

Some of my American friendships provided me with business insights that proved crucial to my long-term success. For example, while I was in graduate school and making plans for my return to B.I.G., I realized that I needed to make some tough decisions about our corporate structure. At the time, we conducted business on a first-come, first-serve basis, making choices in a purely opportunistic fashion without a clear agenda or a system for making decisions in a timely way. I knew that we needed to develop a stronger organizational structure, but I didn't know how to go about it.

I turned for advice to my hunting buddy Ted Herzog, whom I've mentioned earlier. He introduced me to a friend of his named Dale Sorensen, who worked in organizational development for Gulf + Western, the giant global corporation that then owned Paramount Pictures and a number of other major businesses. 'Dale can talk with you about building a corporate structure – the pitfalls to avoid and the key concepts to stress,' Ted said.

Dale and I ended up working together to sketch an effective corporate structure – one that was as flat as possible and clearly designed to avoid the creation of independent, clashing business 'empires'. I still have the document we drew up together, whose value for me and for B.I.G. proved to be enormous.

In those days, I used to travel to the United States about four times a year. Our connections were very enriching and mutually beneficial. Now, unfortunately, those connections have become more tenuous. It is sad and unfortunate that the tragedy of 11 September 2001 caused a temporary rift in communication between the cultures of the Middle East and the United States. Travel to the United States has become more onerous; probing interviews into the plans and motives of honourable business people who are great friends of the country have become very common. I know many business people who have decided, reluctantly, that visiting the United States is now more trouble than it's worth.

B.I.G. still does some business in the United States. Our beverage packaging business is a partnership with Evergreen Packaging, a Memphis-based company that is a former subsidiary of International Paper that was recently sold to a New Zealand company. Therefore our business ties to the United States continue to grow. However, for the foreseeable future, we are balancing our geographic expectations between West and East – the United States and Europe on the one hand, and the Middle East, Africa, the Indian subcontinent and the Far East on the other hand.

For the sake of global cooperation, however, I strongly support the rebuilding of stronger connections between our region and the countries of the West, particularly the United States. It's a heartening sign that thousands of young people from my country are now studying in the United States (and, to a lesser extent, in other parts of the Western world) thanks to well-funded scholarship programmes sponsored by the Saudi Arabian government. Such programmes, which create opportunities for dialogue at the grass-roots level rather than merely between elites and officials, are one key to breaking down the barriers that needlessly separate peoples who can learn so much from one another.

The cross-cultural learning we can do extends far beyond the classroom, of course. It includes simply looking closely at what other countries are doing and drawing comparisons to our own strengths and weaknesses at home. Many times, the only way to see the unique characteristics of your own society clearly is by contrast with a different society.

Dr Haifa Al-Lail, for example, has said that her desire to be a 'change agent' in Saudi Arabia was partly triggered by her observations in the United States. There she saw some cultural, economic and political practices she did not like as well as a few that she considered valuable, such as female empowerment and a thriving, well-regulated civic sector (or 'third sector') of society. Dr Haifa says:

When you get to another country and you see the cultural differences, it can create an internal drive that says we need to bring this to our home. After all, we are an advanced nation with educated people, a rich cultural heritage, and plenty of wealth – so there's no reason why we can't enjoy the same advantages anyone else in the world enjoys.

Today, as a university leader, Dr Haifa is working to adapt the best practices she observed abroad for the benefit of her homeland.

MOATAZ AL-ALFI
Building a multinational corporate culture with a heart

Moataz Al-Alfi is one of the Middle East's most remarkable business leaders. Since 1968, he has been the CEO of Americana Group, where he worked closely with the late Nasser Al-Kharafi. This company, which is one of the world's largest food conglomerates, has grown from 12 employees to today's profile of more than 65,000 employees. It has facilities in 24 countries and is engaged in every stage of the food industry, from growing to processing to packaging to distributing to serving food in restaurants. In 1998, Moataz started another successful enterprise, Egypt Kuwait Holding Company, one of the largest private-equity and venture-capital firms in Egypt.

Moataz is also a notable philanthropist, having turned in later life to focusing much of his attention on contributing resources to benefit the world. He established the Al Alfi Foundation for Human and Social Development to help discover future leaders among Egyptian youth through education and training. He has also founded and helped to lead several other non-profit organizations in the fields of education, healthcare and community development. In fact, this is how I happened to meet him for the first time. Both Moataz and I are committed supporters of the American University in Cairo (AUC), one of the finest institutions of higher education in the region. We met when Moataz visited Jeddah and attended a dinner party in honour of the then AUC president John Gerhart. We clicked immediately, launching a friendship that has only become deeper with the passing years.

As you might imagine, Moataz has many qualities that have contributed to his success, but one of the most significant is his sheer energy. He considers himself on the job up to 20 hours each day. Employees, colleagues, customers, suppliers and other stakeholders from throughout his far-flung corporation have access to him by phone and e-mail practically any time it is necessary. 'I have nothing called weekends', he admits. Vacations are an opportunity to visit farms, factories, processing plants and retailers in cities and towns around the region. It's a long-standing characteristic of his; in fact, he remarks, only half-joking, that the day after his wedding he took his bride to Turkey for their honeymoon – and spent half the day at a shipping facility in Istanbul, checking how food products were being handled.

Moataz tells me that a few hours of sleep at night and an hour of exercise each day are all he needs to recharge his batteries. 'I also like to take short naps – not lying down on a sofa or bed, but just resting my head for 5 or 10 minutes, just long enough to feel refreshed', he says.

Admittedly, not everyone has the physical stamina that Moataz enjoys, but most successful leaders I know – not just in business but in every walk of life – have greater-than-average energy. They are simply willing to *do more* than others – and as a result they achieve more, at higher quality, more quickly than others do.

When it comes to building his company, Moataz is an avid practitioner of cross-cultural learning – which includes learning from business practices that have been successful anywhere in the world:

> *We work with companies from America and Europe, and we invite them to send their employees to stay with us for six or eight weeks at a time. We value having an open pipeline with foreign firms that are in the same line of business as ours – companies like KFC, Hardee's, Carl's Jr., TGI Friday's, and Baskin-Robbins ice cream. Some of the things we've learned from them have been of great practical value. For example, back in 1995, McDonald's was planning to come to our area, which caused us a bit of concern because we are in the hamburger business also. So we sent a group of our managers to work at Hardee's restaurants in the United States for six months to learn exactly how to compete with McDonald's. The result has been that we held our own against McDonald's when it entered our region.*

The story exemplifies the fact that a global business world – and a global industry like fast food – demands global learning. It also demonstrates that, when a business from the MENA region decides to take on the challenge of a powerful multinational rival, it has plenty of opportunity to succeed, providing it does its homework first.

Moataz also believes in environmental stewardship. He invests significant resources in making sure his food companies protect and enhance the local environments in which they operate – treating waste water four separate times before releasing it into the ecosystem, and building their own renewable energy operations so as to avoid releasing carbon into the air. Their pollution-prevention systems are so advanced that government officials visit their facilities to learn from them. 'It's expensive', Moataz says, 'but it's good for the community – and we have to be leaders in nature, just as we are leaders in business.'

Moataz Al-Alfi is one example of the kind of global business leadership the Middle East needs to thrive in the 21st century. Tireless, open to new ideas from everywhere, and committed to social and environmental responsibility, he is building a premier organization that is equipped to compete effectively against rivals from all over the globe.

An open mind: your ticket to continuing education

My own experiences as a student in the West showed me that getting to know other cultures first-hand – engaging rather than disengaging – is the most powerful way to overcome stereotypes and the easy oversimplifications that lead to misunderstandings and mistakes. (As one of my favourite aphorisms reminds us, 'All generalizations are wrong – including this one.')

I'm pleased to report that today's young people from the Middle East are more open, self-confident and adventurous than they were a generation ago, and they are certainly aware of influences from around the globe. However, I believe young people from the region are still a bit more hesitant about engaging with the world than their counterparts in the West – in part because of lack of experience, in part because of strong family traditions that encourage young people to remain close to home. Those powerful family ties are fundamental and valuable, but they need to be balanced with a willingness to reach out to the world (and not just to the West but to every corner of the globe, including the emerging economies of the East, where many of the greatest opportunities for the new century will be found).

Young people can engage with other cultures without becoming rootless citizens of the world who have no home country. The key is to approach the world with the determination to learn from the best of what other cultures have to offer, while retaining the values and principles that make those of us from the Middle East unique, link us to our historic heritage, and represent our special contribution to the world. This includes developing an increased appreciation for the richness of Muslim teachings from the golden age (the 8th to the 13th centuries) regarding business, economics, civil society, ethics and leadership – something B.I.G. has sought to encourage through support of a chair in Islamic economics at Rice University in Houston, Texas.

MAHMOUD EL-GAMAL
Bridging ancient wisdom to contemporary business

For over two decades, I have had a close connection with Rice University in Houston, Texas. It began in the early 1990s when my younger brother was considering attending college in the United States. Because I believe in diversification in education just as I do in investments, I suggested he *not* consider my own alma mater, Rollins College in Florida: 'You can bring a new perspective to our family by attending a different college', I told him. The question was: which college?

One of the friends whose advice I sought was Michel Halbouty, a Lebanese-American oil prospector whom I had met years before through a friend of a friend. A colourful fixture of the roller-coaster Texas oil industry, credited with discovering more than 50 oil and gas fields, Michel came back from bankruptcy to build a great fortune not once but twice, and even wrote a popular book about his adventures called *The Wildcatter*. When I mentioned my brother's quest to Michel, he immediately said, 'You should consider Rice. The president of the university is a friend of mine. I'll call him and we'll have a cup of coffee together.'

The meeting took place as Michel suggested. University president Norman Hackerman and I established a great rapport from the outset. At the end of our conversation, Dr Hackerman said, 'Of course, your brother will need to go through the usual application process, but if he's anything like you I think we'll be happy to have him join us at Rice.' My brother ended up graduating from Rice, and he has always considered it a wonderful choice.

In the years that followed, I kept up my association with Rice. The relationship jumped to a new level later in the 1990s when I noticed the field of Islamic finance beginning to grow in prominence around the world. As a Muslim corporate leader, I was fascinated to see an economic system originally pioneered by Islamic scholars attracting attention from financiers not only in the Arab world but in Europe, North America and elsewhere. However, I also sensed that some of the interest in Islamic finance was driven more by cultural biases than by a deep understanding of the subject and of its potential benefits to society overall. People seemed to be buying the Islamic finance 'brand' without necessarily comprehending its soul. This concerned me, and I began to wonder whether there was something I could do to improve the situation.

After some reflection, I realized that the biggest contribution to this issue could be made by someone with the academic background and knowledge to reshape the general perception of what Islamic finance is really all about. Who better than a respected scholar to take this ancient wisdom and present it in an accurate, useful form for students and practitioners of the present and the future?

I immediately thought of Rice University. I called its then president, Malcolm Gillis, and used my best sales technique to present the idea.

'Dr Gillis,' I said, 'you are an academic leader, while I am in the business sector, but my understanding is that universities compete with one another for students, faculty and resources, just as businesses do. Is that right?'

He agreed.

'Well, then,' I continued, 'what if I were to propose a concept that could allow Rice to be at the forefront in a scholarly field that is growing in importance and popularity around the world?'

'I'd be very interested', he replied. 'What's the concept?'

'I'd like to suggest that Rice University create a chair dedicated to the study of Islamic economics and finance. And I will help arrange the funding to make it possible.'

Dr Gillis liked the idea. Together we wrote up a brief description of the concept to circulate among potential donors. Within six months, we raised the funds needed to endow the new professorship – in fact, I've been told it was the fastest-funded chair in the history of Rice.

Then Rice established a committee to launch an international search for the right individual to occupy this prestigious new academic position. We wanted to find a first-class economist with a passionate interest in Islamic finance, a wealth of knowledge about the inner workings of the modern global financial industry, and a progressive viewpoint that would enable him or her to communicate to a wide audience of 21st-century scholars and practitioners. More than just a fine scholar, we wanted someone capable of building bridges – between disciplines, between cultures, even between eras.

In time, the choice centred on Mahmoud El-Gamal, a native of Cairo, Egypt, who was then a tenured professor of economics at the highly respected University of Wisconsin at Madison. Dr Gillis asked me to try to sway his decision. I met with Mahmoud in the United States and talked with him about this opportunity. I also invited him to Saudi Arabia, where we spent two or three days together in the holy city of Medinah. After much discussion and consideration on his part, he finally said, 'I'll do it.'

Mahmoud joined the faculty at Rice in 1998, and he has served the university, its students and the world of scholarship with great distinction ever since. He has also become a friend of mine; we meet annually in Madinah during his winter break, where we enjoy a period of reflection and thoughtful conversation about topics of mutual interest.

Mahmoud El-Gamal exemplifies one important kind of leader in today's global world. Although he recently served a stint as chairman of Rice's economics department, he does not exercise leadership primarily as a manager, administrator, or supervisor of other people. Instead, he aspires to be a 'thought leader', someone who influences the ideas, knowledge and values of other people through his teaching, his speaking, his research and his writings.

His students at Rice include many from the countries of the MENA region along with a large number from the United States, Europe and elsewhere who are eager to hear his perspectives on Islamic finance as well as the other economic subjects he teaches, while his writings include articles in scholarly journals, opinion columns in newspapers and magazines, and a highly respected textbook, *Islamic Finance: Law, Economics, and Practice*, published in 2006 by Cambridge University Press.

In today's global world, thought leaders like Mahmoud help to shape the way the world views their subject areas, and they participate in setting the intellectual agenda for future generations of thinkers, researchers and students. In particular, Mahmoud views his mission as placing the field of Islamic finance within the broader context of economics, law, sociology and religion – an integrated, interdisciplinary approach that emphasizes what scholars and practitioners from many related fields can learn from one another.

Mahmoud recalls:

> *I started my career as a mainstream economist who happens to be Muslim, but as the years went on I saw, both inside and outside academia, the rise of Islamism,*

driven by the desire of many people to live their lives in accordance with religion. The growth of Islamic finance is largely related to this broader social trend, and for me it raised some fascinating and important questions. How can Muslim societies be authentic to Islamic tradition while integrating with the modern world in a way that will allow them to be competitive? Does being authentically Muslim mean we have to go back to the Middle Ages in designing our business and financial practices?

Mahmoud's answers to these questions are not shared by all scholars and practitioners of Islamic finance, but they are growing in influence and acceptance over time. In his view, it's important for contemporary Muslims to interpret Islamic tradition in ways that are consistent with the times they live in, just as Muslims in the medieval period interpreted the revelation in ways that were compatible with their world.

Some assume that Islamic finance must mean rejecting any business practice that was not generally accepted in the Islamic world of the Middle Ages, but Mahmoud's research has taught him that, in fact, Muslim business leaders in medieval times were very happy to adapt innovations and systems they encountered from the non-Islamic cultures with which they came into contact. 'Islamic tradition evolved by accepting innovations that were made by others', he says. 'Learning from the best practices of others is, in fact, part of our heritage, so I argue that we should not examine the rules and prohibitions we've inherited from ancient times in rigid, ritualistic fashion but instead focus on their economic substance.'

An example is the practice of mortgage lending, which was unknown in the Muslim world of the Middle Ages yet is an essential element of modern property finance. A 'ritualistic' interpretation of Islamic finance might suggest that mortgage lending should be forbidden to Muslims, but Mahmoud suggests that we should focus instead on the underlying economic and religious substance of mortgage lending:

The central intent of Islamic jurisprudence in this area is to avoid severe indebtedness and the risk of bankruptcy that it brings. All religious restrictions are for human benefit. If I am a borrower, I should be guided by ethical constraints: I shouldn't overextend myself; I should avoid buying into a property bubble; I must be prudent about going into excessive debt and thereby endangering myself and my family. And if I am a lender I have a similar ethical duty to prevent others from taking on unnecessary risk, even if encouraging them to do so might enrich me in the short term.

If these ethical, social and moral rules are followed, there's no reason a devout Muslim can't participate in well-structured mortgage lending – just as Muslims from the Middle Ages participated fully, and successfully, in the financial systems of their day.

As a highly respected scholar from the Muslim world who is addressing concerns of importance to everyone in the contemporary world – and in his role as the faculty adviser to the Muslim Students Association at Rice University – Mahmoud is often asked for advice about how young people from our region can successfully bridge the gap between traditional culture and modern life. He says:

My advice is always the same. Find what you're good at, and find what you like. Then, if you can carve out a career in an intersection between those two things, you're a very lucky person. I happened to find that intersection outside of Egypt, here in the United States, where life as a Muslim has its own opportunities and challenges. But life abroad may not be the best choice for others of an academic inclination. I myself would have been very interested in pursuing an academic career back in Egypt if the right opportunities had been available. By the same token, if I were from Turkey, I would have liked to work at a Turkish university, and if I were from South Korea I would have liked to work at a South Korean university. I have students who have followed that path and found great satisfaction in it.

The real answer to any career question must be custom-made for the individual. The choices you make must grow from within.

In his life and work, Mahmoud El-Gamal serves as a bridge between differing cultures and disciplines. He helps students of global finance as well as financial practitioners from around the world understand the ethical and moral traditions of Islam, showing how ancient principles of integrity, compassion and justice are still relevant and essential today. At the same time, he helps young people from the Middle East learn how they can combine a deep commitment to their religious and cultural heritage with successful careers in today's competitive global business arena. Thanks to Unknown Leaders like Mahmoud, the gaps between old and new, religious and secular, and East and West are becoming a little narrower and a little easier to cross, bringing benefits to people and institutions from all around the world.

Traditional culture enriches contemporary life

Paradoxically, engaging with the larger world can actually be the best way of coming to understand and appreciate your own heritage. Recall the work of Asma Siddiki, whose Heritage Summers educational programme for young people we described in Chapter 1. Motivated to help young people of Muslim backgrounds learn more about their rich cultural background, Dr Asma hit upon the idea of bringing them to leading universities in England where they could learn about the glories of Arab history in a global context. These young students develop a much richer understanding of the unique contributions of Muslim culture to the world at large by seeing those contributions against the backdrop of European, Asian, North American and world cultures.

It's a fascinating paradox: the more one understands the cultures of all humanity, and both the common threads and the dramatic differences between those cultures and the specifically Muslim elements native to the MENA region, the more knowledgeably and proudly one can embrace one's own background. In effect, becoming a citizen of the world can help you to become an even more committed and patriotic citizen of Saudi Arabia, Egypt, Lebanon, Morocco or whatever country you belong to.

Developing global leaders in the MENA region is not about 'Westernizing' or 'Americanizing' the Middle East. It's about making the best of the globalizing process that is inevitable and that is already under way – and doing it in a form that maximizes the value of the region's unique and remarkable heritage.

8

The art of nurturing leaders

In the quest to create the next generation of leaders for the Middle East, there are important roles to play for both the private and public sectors. In this chapter, I'll describe some of the many educational trends currently operating in the MENA region. I'll discuss how business leaders – including those at B.I.G. – are becoming involved in advocating educational reforms as well as training future leaders among their own employees, and I'll share some ideas about what the region's societies can do to drive further improvement in educational systems, so that the region will be better positioned to meet the leadership demands of the coming decades.

From classrooms to boardrooms

Schools, colleges and universities have always been breeding grounds for leadership talent. Unfortunately, in the MENA region, the educational infrastructure needed for turning out large number of leaders equipped for the challenges of the 21st century is not yet fully in place, although some countries in the region, especially the Gulf countries, have recently moved forward with reform at a rapid pace, while countries like Lebanon have long been on the cutting edge of educational leadership. This is partly because the region has grown so much, so quickly, and in particular because we have such vast numbers of bright young men and women eager for training and learning. It's also related to the continuing strong influence of traditional ideas on educational curricula. The region's schools tend to emphasize lectures, rote learning, memorization, and high-stakes exams that require students to regurgitate facts; they give short shrift to dialogue, debate, analysis, interpretation, and assignments that call for self-expression and originality. The traditional structure was adequate in the past century, but in today's more demanding world students must develop the high-order thinking and creative skills that employers around the world are demanding. School systems in Saudi Arabia and elsewhere in the region are beginning to make the necessary adjustments, but they need to accelerate the process; otherwise there will be a mismatch between opportunity and preparation.

So one of the key challenges the region's societies face in the next few decades is the building of an educational system that is the equal of any in the world – or preferably even better!

Fortunately, many of the region's most talented leaders are actively engaged in building the educational programmes and institutions needed for the coming years. Moataz Al-Alfi, for example, while continuing to manage his international food business, now devotes much of his time and energy to the work of the Al-Alfi Foundation in supporting educational programmes for talented young Egyptians. This work is under way on many fronts. The foundation supports the building of schools in rural districts of Egypt where none are available, and provides computers for classrooms filled with students who have never seen one – along with electrical generators to provide the energy to power them. It also conducts advanced training programmes for elementary school teachers, hiring educational experts who have identified the most effective teaching techniques to pass their insights on for use in the classroom. (Microsoft founder Bill Gates is involved in similar programmes in the United States.)

Driven by the conviction that science, mathematics and technology will be keys to the future economic growth of Egypt and the rest of the Middle East, the Al-Alfi Foundation is also developing projects to identify and nurture talent in these fields. In partnership with the Center for Talented Youth run by Johns Hopkins University in Baltimore, Maryland, the foundation has created a programme that provides very bright boys and girls, aged 6 to 12, with special after-school and summer classes in science and mathematics. The hope is that a few of these talented youngsters will grow into the scientific geniuses – the Nobel Prize winners – of the future, inspiring still more Egyptian youth to pursue careers in these important but currently neglected disciplines.

The improvement of educational opportunities at the higher educa-tion level (college and above) is equally important. Inspiring work is being done by academic leaders like Dr Haifa Al-Lail at Effat University, often with support from education officials in govern-ment, experts in non-profit organizations and foundations, and business organizations that understand the need for well-trained leaders in the region.

My personal conviction is that giving freer rein to private individuals and organizations in the educational sphere, with the right govern-ment oversight, is likely to help accelerate improvements in the school systems that will benefit both students and society as a whole. In the MENA region, we continue to place numerous obstacles in the way of privately run educational institutions; these private institutions are recognized, but they are treated with scepticism, and they take a back seat to government-run systems. I would like to see a level playing field between public and private educational institutions. In fields from science and technology to medicine, we've seen mile-stone achievements driven by experimentation in the private sector. The same may be possible in education.

One of the initiatives that we're very proud of at B.I.G. is our support for the Ambassadors Program at Effat University. This is a specially designed leadership programme that operates on the 'cascade model': teachers share their knowledge with students, who then 'cascade' this learning to younger students. The process enhances the students' leadership abilities and strengthens their skills by combining learning, doing and teaching in a self-reinforcing system.

Under the Ambassadors Program, students are developed in four key areas – academic, personal, professional and social. Advanced students work in the Independent Learning Center at the university, where they provide peer tutoring services in such subject areas as mathematics, physics and foreign languages. The students also have the opportunity to work for pay in various departments of the university. In many cases, it's their first responsible job outside the home, offering an invaluable experience of meeting deadlines, prioritizing tasks, accepting responsibility, communicating effectively, and practising ethical behaviour at work.

Thirty students receive scholarships through the Ambassadors Program annually. Each has been chosen based on academic and character criteria developed by Effat University, as well as personal leadership qualities. Based on the feedback we've received from both staff and students, we think some of the finest young leaders from the next generation of Saudi women will be emerging from the Ambassadors Program in the coming years, exemplifying the six leadership traits I described in Chapter 4.

Another educational programme I am proud to support is the Al-Banawi Scholarship for Personal Development, administered by Franklin College in Lugano, Switzerland. This scholarship is designed to meet a specific need that I became aware of during my own years as a student abroad: namely, the need for mentoring and counselling to help a young person adjust to the challenges of life in a very different culture from the one in which he or she grew up.

In Chapter 7 I've spoken glowingly of the benefits to be gained from an educational encounter with a foreign culture. I'm a great believer in the value of this experience, particularly in today's closely inter-woven global community, but study abroad also has its risk, particu-larly for students who lack prior experience in living or travelling far from home. Separated not just from the sheltering arms of their family but also from the familiar rules, habits, values and assump-tions that shape their home culture, students sometimes become psychologically and emotionally disoriented.

The Al-Banawi Scholarship for Personal Development is an attempt to address this problem at one of my own alma maters. Franklin College is a fine Swiss-based higher education institution that attracts students from around the world, including many from the MENA region. Scholarship recipients will be chosen on the basis of academic excellence, leadership potential and financial need. In exchange for a generous financial grant to help cover tuition costs, scholarship recipients will be asked to serve as mentors to international students who are showing signs of academic difficulty due to maladjustment. With guidance from the dean of the college, the mentors will help their mentees deal with such common issues as time management, self-discipline, study habits, health and fitness, social pressures, homesickness, and adjustment to college life.

My hope is that this programme will help ensure that young people from the MENA region and even other regions who have the oppor-tunity to study abroad will be able to take full advantage of the benefits this experience offers, without falling prey to any of the temptations that might otherwise short-circuit their academic advancement.

It's also important to support efforts to upgrade the higher educa-tion opportunities available in the region. There's no better way to spend some of the wealth generated by oil revenues than by investing it in first-rate colleges, universities, graduate programmes, and pro-fessional schools in every discipline, from medicine and engineering to business and law. Brilliant young students from the Gulf nations and other countries in the region shouldn't feel that they have to travel to Europe or the United States to enjoy up-to-the-minute education; we need to ensure that equally great training is available in classrooms in the region. I'd like to see the day when the flow of Middle Eastern students to colleges and universities in California, New York and the UK is matched by an equal flow of US, British and European students into colleges in cities like Jeddah, Cairo, Istanbul and Dubai.

Building a truly great modern educational infrastructure is a major project that will take decades, not just years, but in some parts of the region a number of pieces of that infrastructure are already in place. My friend the banker Hisham Ezz Al-Arab was educated at Cairo University in the 1970s, which then was a world-class institution that boasted a number of Nobel Prize winners on its staff. Sadly, it has lost a bit of its lustre since then, but there is no reason it cannot be restored to its past prominence. All that's required is a renewed vision, proper management, support from government and the private sector, and the will to make it happen. The same is true of other universities elsewhere in the Middle East.

Fortunately, impressive advances in higher education are now taking shape in many places throughout our region. My friend Nabil Alyousuf, whose work with the Dubai government was described in Chapter 2, has been among the leaders who helped to create the Dubai School of Government (DSG) in partnership with the Lee Kuan Yew School of Public Policy in Singapore. Nabil explains:

> *The philosophy behind the creation of DSG was to address a regional weakness at the policy-making level. People in government tended to be purely bureaucrats who'd grown through the ranks because of seniority. Others were people who were friends of friends and received appointments on this basis. In both cases, they often lacked the background and education needed to develop the right policies and make the right decisions for the long-term growth and progress of the region.*

Since then, DSG has brought to the region experts of policy making from around the world, providing knowledge, models and tools for planning and decision making to government officials, entrepreneurs and corporate managers in the region. More recently, it has focused on leadership development and capacity building among policy makers in the UAE and Gulf region.

Nabil also helped to start the Mohammed Bin Rashid Leadership Development Program, which takes young people from Dubai who are judged to have distinct high potential from both the public sector and the private sector and put them in a two-year programme to develop their leadership skills. The goal is to create a pipeline of leaders for the Dubai emirate, and graduates of the programme are already emerging as among the Emirates' most promising young talents in government, business and the non-profit sector.

Closing the human capital gap

Some might be surprised by the number of programmes I've mentioned that involve businesses supporting or even initiating educational reforms and advances. Isn't education traditionally a matter for government to manage? That's true to an extent. But like many corporate leaders, I've become convinced that our biggest economic dilemma – in the MENA region, and in other parts of the world as well – is not about property, energy prices, health care costs, raw materials or any other matter. It's the vast and growing gap between the human capital we need to transform our societies into the high-powered 21st-century value-creating engines they ought to be and the amount of human capital we are actually producing. Of course, the reason for this gap is that 'human capital' doesn't include just raw numbers of people – far more importantly, it refers to the talent, intelligence, skill and creative capacity of those people.

This is why I, like many of my colleagues in the business world, am an enthusiastic supporter of business-sponsored projects to improve our educational infrastructure and to provide greater access to it for more people than ever before. And I think that, as a society, we can and should be doing more.

One concept I advocate would be for the government to create a multi-billion-dollar human capital fund (HCF) for my home country of Saudi Arabia. It would be the first such fund in the region and would, I hope, serve as a model for similar funds in many other countries. The primary goals of the fund would be to help build private educational infrastructure and to provide scholarships, loans, college allowances and other forms of support to young people in search of higher education. The fund could also provide financial support directly to educational programmes – for example, it would provide the necessary start-up resources needed to launch an institution, including land for building the institution on a low-cost, long-term lease, or it might offer an institution 'soft loans' sufficient to cover operating costs until the institution is self-supporting. Colleges and universities would be eligible, but so would vocational programmes, technological training, professional certification courses, and other kinds of worthwhile post-high-school programmes.

In my vision of the HCF, the government would finance the fund for the benefit of educational institutions in the private sector. Demand would be driven not by decisions from a high-level government agency or commission, but by gauging the interests of millions of individual students following their passions and career aspirations. I think this is the right model for public–private partnerships in education. The government should create the most effective climate and regulatory environment, setting high-quality standards for curricula and teachers while defining a human capital agenda for the entire nation. For its part, the private sector should provide the entrepreneurial spirit and market orientation that lead to innovation and efficiency. In this model, students, teachers and employers are viewed as customers, giving private sector educational institutions an opportunity to bridge the gap between what teachers and students want and what employers are looking for.

I envision that the availability of funds through the HCF would, in turn, spark an entrepreneurial boom in the building of educational infrastructure. Both for-profit businesses and non-profit organizations could decide to create schools, institutes, training centres, academies and colleges dedicated to particular forms of learning, focusing on specialized technical skills in sectors that are crucial to the future of the region, such as energy, retail, hospitality, health care, financial services, transportation and manufacturing. These will increase the per capita income of the people by teaching them real value-added skills in sectors that will help sustain the transformation of our region and improve our people's quality of life.

The key is that we view the activities of the HCF not as commercial transactions measured in terms of immediate profit, but rather as the ultimate investment in our future generations.

I believe that a public–private partnership of this kind can create a boom in skills development training that will help close the yawning human capital gap, serve the nation for decades to come, and become a model for other countries that have similar issues.

Developing leadership from the ranks

Schools, colleges and universities play an important role in educating the young people who will be the leaders of tomorrow, but leadership isn't something you can learn solely from a textbook or even from a classroom discussion. It's something you learn by doing – in the trenches. For this reason, businesses themselves have a huge influence in shaping the rising generation of leaders. The way in which companies recruit, select, train and nurture talented young men and women helps to determine the kinds of leaders who will serve at the helm of various enterprises two decades or so down the line – and that, in turn, helps to shape the kind of economy we'll live in.

Many companies take their educational mission so seriously that they launch their own internal training programmes, some of them quite ambitious. On a global level, the model is probably GE, whose campus in Crotonville, New York is famous around the world as a centre for business education. GE managers come to Crotonville from every continent to learn the latest secrets of management, marketing, finance, strategy and leadership from other GE executives as well as from professors from some of the world's leading business schools.

Moataz Al-Alfi's Egypt Kuwait Holding Company has joined GE and other corporate leaders in establishing its own training centres for rising young business leaders:

> *We have schools in Egypt and Dubai where we send young managers that we are preparing for greater responsibilities. Our approach is an interesting one. In addition to having them take classes at our schools, we also require them to become teachers there for a six-month period. We find that teaching a subject like strategy, logistics, marketing or management is the best way to master that subject. And we also believe strongly that teaching is a crucial element in all leadership. If you want to create an effective working team, you need to know how to teach. If you don't know how to teach, you don't know how to manage, so we make sure all of our managers have some teaching experience and skill.*

Other companies in the MENA region have taken on the challenge of spreading ideas, information and knowledge about their own industries to local youth – in effect, preparing the work force they will need to fuel their next stage of growth and development. These businesses have come to recognize that they can't just hire college- or university-educated students and assume a basic knowledge of how their industry works. Instead, companies sometimes have to undertake their own educational programmes, especially when they are trying to introduce a new way of doing business that is not familiar to everyone in the region. Learning is everybody's business – especially in a time and place when change is the rule, not the exception.

HANI KHOJA
Developing leaders from the ground level up

Hani Khoja is founder and director of Elixir, a management consulting firm whose vision is to help local companies, governments, non-profit organizations and individuals succeed globally via creative strategic solutions. He and his company are also a fine example of how smart businesses are developing systems for growing the leaders of the future.

I was fortunate enough to meet Hani while working with my colleagues at B.I.G. on planning our corporate social responsibility (CSR) initiative. At first, we considered a variety of possible social focuses. After much reflection, I realized that the single most important factor influencing our region, both individually and as a society, is the profile and character of the leadership that emerges from the ranks. With this as inspiration, we at B.I.G. decided to embark on a number of social responsibility programmes focused on the nurturing of young leaders. We then knew that we needed the help of a knowledgeable outside consultant to design and implement the complete programme, and a friend of one of our board members introduced me to Hani. It has turned out to be a very opportune connection.

Under Hani's leadership, Elixir has become one of the most successful consulting firms in the Middle East. However, Hani's path to the pinnacle of the consulting profession was not a direct one. His first job after business school was at the global consumer goods company Procter & Gamble (P&G), where he expected to spend his entire career. It turned out that Hani's 12 years at P&G became a long apprenticeship for the work he was meant to do.

After a stint in management in P&G's Brussels office, he returned to Saudi Arabia, where he rose steadily through the leadership ranks. However, he says:

> *As you go up the ranks of a corporation, you tend to do more of the same tasks, although you do them much better the more experience you have. So at some point I began to feel a bit bored, and I ended up doing a lot of after-hours consulting with friends and family that had businesses. For example, one person opened a hospital and needed advice, so I tried to help him out. Another owned a retail outlet and was having inventory management issues, so I went and helped him out. I soon found that my advice was actually making an impact. And then some of my friends said, 'Why don't you just do this full time?'*
>
> *That was the first time I actually faced the question of leaving P&G, and after a period of serious thought and reflection it led to my co-founding Elixir.*

Hani deliberately avoided the obvious, predictable path when he helped to launch the company:

> *For me, coming out of P&G, it would have been natural to specialize in fast-moving consumer goods, since that is the area in which P&G is deservedly famous. But we didn't want to be labelled and perhaps restricted to one kind of business. So for our first three to four years, we purposely focused on every other type of marketing – corporate marketing, building materials, hospitals, health care, cement ready-mix, real estate – and in this way gradually built a wide-ranging reputation.*

Hani's story reminds us of an important lesson for any would-be leader: be prepared to change direction in mid-career if that is the right step for you, and don't be afraid to make the unconventional or less-than-obvious choice! Sometimes breaking out from the norm can lead to a more rewarding path – one that will better enable you to discover, develop and fully express the leader inside you.

Today Elixir is pursuing a vision that centres on creating economic growth and opportunity not just for individual leaders and their companies but for cities, countries and the entire Middle East region – a big vision that calls forth extraordinary efforts from Hani and from all of those who work with him. Every project that Hani and his team accept must fit into that overarching vision. This shared sense of purpose animates the entire organization, as you can palpably sense when you walk into one of Elixir's offices or spend time talking with one of Hani's brilliant young associates.

Like other great companies, Elixir is marked by the seriousness with which it approaches the task of grooming leaders. Hani speaks with admiration about the talent development system he observed at Procter & Gamble:

> *P&G is a great place to develop leaders, because they give you responsibility from day one. There's a pressure to deliver, and it's an up-or-out culture. If you deliver, you get promoted, but if you don't deliver you get asked to leave very politely.*

At the same time, P&G has a promote-from-within culture, so you would never find yourself suddenly working for some outsider after you've been diligently working your way up the ladder. When a leader must be found, it's always somebody within the organization that has gotten the culture from day one, which means they definitely trust you, and they trust their recruiting system to attract the top talent. And then they give this top talent the autonomy to go and get things done, and the freedom and the courage to make mistakes, learn from their mistakes, and then develop their capabilities for leadership. All in all, it's an excellent culture to develop your raw talent.

In order to develop the leadership potential within every Elixir associate, Hani Khoja runs the company in a highly collaborative fashion. Consulting assignments at the firm are generally handled by small, close-knit teams of three, four or five people, working intensively with a handful of contacts at the client organization. This structure is designed to ensure that everyone involved in a project is aware of all the details, so that whatever needs to be done on a given day can be handled quickly and efficiently – there's no time wasted in waiting for one central authority figure to give the nod. Leadership may shift from one person to another as the needs of the project dictate. In fact, on a particular case, Hani himself may work under a younger consultant for a specific assignment if the junior person has specialized knowledge or experience that confer a leadership edge.

Even the physical environment at Elixir is designed to encourage collaboration. Nobody has a private office. Instead, everyone shares an open space with room to work, technology hook-ups, whiteboards for note-taking, and other facilities. Under the 'hotelling' system, anyone who needs a place to work can claim it for as long as they need it; people working together on a project simply find two or three spots that are close to one another so they can talk as needed. (In the Jeddah, Saudi Arabia office – one of three Elixir locations – seating is around a giant open desk in the shape of a figure of eight, perhaps better described as resembling the infinity symbol from mathematics.) A small conference room to one side provides private space when needed for a meeting with a client. Otherwise, everyone is together, able to see and hear one another at all times – an approach that tends to level hierarchies, encourage instantaneous communication, and provoke constant exchange of ideas: collaborative leadership at its best.

The best way to learn to lead is by actually doing it – one task, one meeting, one project at a time. The collaborative style of management at Elixir gives everyone on the team a turn in the pilot's seat. This ensures that the next generation of leaders for the company will be well prepared to take the helm when their time arrives.

Leadership in motion and B.I.G.

B.I.G. takes leadership development just as seriously as Procter & Gamble, GE and other world-class organizations, but we tailor it to our own corporate culture and region. We constantly ask how our leadership programme can help improve skills and knowledge and provide opportunity and exposure but without taking away from our corporate values of entrepreneurship and balance between progress and regional priorities. In fact, B.I.G. has made the nurturing of leadership an explicit part of its corporate purpose: 'To be true to our core as custodians of wealth and careers; valued always as best in class'. Those two goals – that is, to be custodians of wealth and careers – are sometimes at opposite sides of the equation; we can't pursue one at the expense of the other. But we take the challenge of nurturing the careers of the next generation of leaders very seriously – just as seriously as we take the challenge of boosting revenues and profits for our share owners. We believe B.I.G. can be a model for other companies that are concerned with ensuring a strong set of leaders to whom we can entrust our future.

The process begins with our hiring decisions. We consciously strive to identify individuals who embody the six qualities of leadership – not just people with technical skills.

One day several years ago, our head of human resources came to me with a typical dilemma: 'We've got two candidates for the same job, and they're both good. We're undecided over which one to choose. What do you think?'

After looking over the CVs, which were indeed very comparable, I said, 'Hire the fire.' Now 'Hire the fire!' has become a company motto and a principle we live by: whichever candidate has the fire in him or her is the person we need to give the opportunity to. This leads to some good advice for young people starting out: find the fire within yourself, and fuel it. It is the starting point for everything you hope to achieve.

When making hiring decisions, we also look for an element of maturity. The quality of maturity allows us to take things in stride, to resist the tendency to exaggerate other people's actions and reactions. Sometimes our emotional responses blind us from what really is at hand and cloud our perceptions of the situation. So I like to see that a job candidate has the ability to take a step back in times of turmoil and say, 'Let's assess this right – without letting emotions distract us from our goal.' This level of maturity allows an individual to be flexible, able to deal with a particular situation or opportunity as circumstances require rather than being tossed by the waves of emotion. True leadership demands maturity, and more so as one's career develops.

We continue to focus on leadership as young people rise through our organization. At B.I.G., we are committed to designating 20 per cent of our employees as current or future leaders. Then our goal is deliberately to nurture them – not mainly through training programmes but by carefully placing them in the right positions and rapidly giving them significant responsibilities. We gradually increase the responsibility and the pressure, trying to gauge when individuals will be ready for it and 'throwing them in at the deep end' expeditiously.

We also introduce experiences that get our future leaders ready for upper management tasks – for example, by bringing young managers into meetings with executives several levels above them and having them do brief presentations, just to get them accustomed to the challenge of open platform speaking, of doing their homework and of thinking on their feet. Having an opinion isn't enough. Opinions are like mobile phones – everyone has one! To be worthwhile, an opinion must be backed up with facts or well-thought-out arguments and defended clearly and persuasively. We try to train our young leaders to do this in the best way possible – through real-life experience.

In addition, we move our potential leaders into various jobs so they can learn about the different aspects of our business. That way, if they eventually join the top management of the company, they will have personal experiences that help them understand the challenges and pressures of manufacturing, logistics, sales and all the other disciplines and functions of our industry, as well as the many internal and external forces that drive a business toward success or failure.

Today, business education isn't only about earning a degree. It's fundamentally about developing new skills – whether through a university programme, an apprenticeship, an online course, an intensive two-week seminar, a brief assignment in a different sector, or whatever. The paper credential matters, but the skill matters more!

The final, crucial element in encouraging young business people to exercise their leadership skills is to allow them to spread their wings – to hand them real responsibilities and watch how they respond. Here's a striking example. About 10 years ago, one of our managers from Lebanon who helped to run part of B.I.G.'s beverage packaging business attended a meeting that I chaired. I didn't know him up close – he was not one of my direct reports – but we like to give our people an opportunity to speak up. Sometime during the meeting, he came out with a surprising assertion: 'There's an important part of the world that we are not doing business in that is ready to experience big growth in the coming years!'

This got my attention. 'What part of the world are you talking about?' I asked.

'I'm talking about North Africa – from Tunisia to Morocco', he replied. I probed for a few details, and as the manager spoke it was obvious that he had done his homework. He had studied the region, examined the business climate, considered the evolving demographics, and recognized the potential for B.I.G. to have a significant business impact.

I realized that opportunity was staring me in the face. 'Pack your bags!' I told the young man. 'We're sending you to Tunisia, with the mandate to establish our presence in the region.' Today, B.I.G. has a meaningful presence in North Africa – in fact, the countries that manager identified represent a sizeable part of our beverage packaging business. And after building his own career to new heights of achievement at B.I.G., he has since moved on to further success at another company – with our gratitude and admiration.

I think this story offers two powerful lessons. One is about the importance of being open to good ideas, no matter where they come from. I could easily have stifled the young manager's enthusiasm by saying to him, 'Please write a report about your idea and submit it to your boss. We have to follow proper management channels.' His idea might have been delayed by months or years – or it might have died on the vine. Instead, we grabbed it and ran with it, and everyone involved became a winner.

The other lesson, of course, is that young people can sometimes exhibit amazing leadership skills – provided they have an opportunity to use them. I urge business leaders to occasionally allow their talented young people to jump in 'over their heads'. You may sometimes be disappointed by the results – but more often than you expect you will be amazed and delighted!

Mentorship: a powerful tool for advancement

At B.I.G., we also believe in other powerful tools for grooming leaders, including mentorship. It's a practice that most people are familiar with but that is sometimes misunderstood – and sometimes poorly managed.

The best mentor is not necessarily someone who is in the direct chain of command or authority for the mentee. Rather than regularly turning to your supervisor or boss as a mentor, consider relying on someone with equal experience and wisdom who works in a different department, a different company or even a different industry. This approach provides several advantages: it eliminates the possibility of favouritism when a promotion, pay increase or other coveted benefit is up for grabs; it provides the mentee with a fresh perspective on the challenges of the job rather than a mere repetition of the same advice he or she hears every day; and it creates the possibility of meeting a new constellation of individuals who may be helpful in the mentee's later career.

My friend Ghazi Binzagr says that, in the merchant family in which he grew up, it was customary for the young men to be mentored not by their fathers but by their uncles. This expresses the same idea – it removes the mentor–mentee relationship from the stresses that naturally accompany the father–son dynamic, and gives the mentee a different voice to turn to in times of uncertainty or difficulty.

SAMEER AL ANSARI
The art of mentorship through tests and trials

Sameer Al Ansari is founder and former CEO of Dubai International Capital, an investment firm focused mainly on private equity holdings throughout the Middle East and Europe, as well as former CEO of SHUAA Capital, the leading regional investment bank. I first met Sameer after my colleagues and I at B.I.G. decided to explore the possibility of taking our company public some time in the future. This naturally required that we zoom in on an investment banking firm to work with and, just as important, an individual investment banker to whom we were willing to entrust the assignment of shepherding us through the enormously significant and complex process of becoming a public company one day.

The city of Dubai, the hub of the region, offered a wealth of choices among many well-regarded and highly knowledgeable investment banking firms. B.I.G. held a 'beauty contest' among a number of firms that expressed an interest in working with us, and SHUAA Capital was one of the half-dozen finalists. Sameer Al Ansari's personal qualities played a major role in tilting towards his firm. His passion, his dedication to his work, his commitment to the economic future of the region, and the skill with which he'd developed an impressive team of colleagues – all these helped his bank stand out from the competition.

In time, Sameer stepped down from his CEO role, preferring to put his years of hands-on experience to use in a more independent entrepreneurial role. That certainly didn't end his connection with B.I.G. We invited Sameer to become a member of our board, and he has quickly become one of our greatest assets. The respect he commands throughout the banking and financial services industries, his business acumen, and his rich network of contacts at the highest levels of industry all make him the kind of leader any company would be thrilled to be associated with.

Having attained these remarkable heights in the business arena of his choice, Sameer Al Ansari has not forgotten the support of those who helped him achieve his current status. In fact, he still speaks with admiration and appreciation about his first mentor – a managing partner at the accounting firm of Ernst & Young (E&Y) named Edward Quinlan.

Sameer began to learn from Quinlan when he was quite young and filled with the usual medley of emotions that young people experience. He was ambitious, impatient and eager to advance, but also afflicted by doubts about his abilities and uncertain about whether other people believed in him. 'When you're young like that', Sameer says, 'you need someone to hold your hand on this journey of uncertainty. You need a mentor.' Ed Quinlan played that role for young Sameer.

One of the key lessons Quinlan provided was to teach Sameer about the importance of being a team player, willing and able to learn from anyone in the company. 'Most of the young people I've worked with,' Sameer says, 'are more comfortable doing things on their own. The work remains within boundaries and easy to define – whereas working closely with others can be much harder to control.'

Quinlan not only encouraged Sameer to practise the art of team playing, but he even *forced* him to do it at times when Sameer was reluctant. For example, during Sameer's tenure at E&Y's Dubai office, Quinlan decided to send him to perform a quality check on the work of another E&Y office, which at that time was widely considered to be a problem spot.

Sameer objected. 'But that's a complete waste of my time', he said. 'I know they're not doing a good job, and we've got important clients in Dubai and Abu Dhabi that I would rather be seeing. Why do you want me to go to another office?'

Quinlan stuck to his guns, and when Sameer actually spent two weeks in the troubled office he found himself learning a host of new skills he might otherwise have waited years to experience. He learned first-hand how to deal with problematic banks with poor documentation and difficult management, how to manage in a messy business environment, and how to win support for improvements from managers and colleagues. Sameer helped fix the problems in the affiliate office – but he also discovered that he benefited even more from the process than his colleagues did.

In a similar vein, Quinlan drove Sameer to learn the art of delegating – one of the more difficult things for many young leaders to do. As young professionals develop their technical knowledge and skill, it is easy simply to take on more and more tasks, relying solely on one's own abilities to get the work done to the highest possible standard. The problem with this approach is that it limits the amount you can accomplish, since even the most talented and energetic person can work only so many hours in the day. The only way to expand one's capacities is to learn to delegate – to teach others how to help with parts of a project, to motivate and supervise them appropriately, and to fit all the parts of the job together into a coherent whole. Quinlan showed young Sameer how to do this, helping him to develop trust in his associates and knowledge of how to lead them effectively through completion of a complex project.

Even as he pushed Sameer to stretch his abilities, Ed Quinlan also encouraged and supported him. When Sameer had doubts about his abilities and even wondered whether he was in the right career, Quinlan encouraged him. When Sameer made mistakes that cost E&Y time and money, Quinlan didn't berate him but rather urged him to turn the negative into a positive: 'We all make mistakes. Now your job is to learn from them.'

The story of Sameer Al Ansari and Edward Quinlan illustrates the fact that there are times when a relationship with a mentor involves a certain amount of friction. Mentorship is not only about the mentor encouraging you and patting you on the back; it's also, at times, about the mentor forcing you to do things that you think you don't want to do or don't need to do. If you choose a mentor wisely, there will be times when the mentor pushes you out of your comfort zone – and that can be both a painful and a very valuable experience.

Today, Sameer looks back on his years at E&Y and says, 'There were times when I just hated Edward and the way he was bullying me and pushing me. But if it wasn't for that, I would never have been able to achieve the things I did, and that's why I'm eternally grateful to Edward for his role in my life.'

Now, of course, Sameer is playing a similar mentorship role for the young people who are lucky enough to be his friends and associates. In this way, the wisdom of leadership is passed on from one generation to the next, leaving behind a rich legacy of endurance, success and achievement.

At B.I.G., we've also discovered that one key to nurturing effective leaders is putting them in the right niche. When an employee repeatedly fumbles the ball, we evaluate the person's character, effort and skills. If all three are sound, we ask, 'Have we put this person in a position where we are drawing on his or her weaknesses rather than strengths?' It's easy to sack someone – it's harder to find the right niche for the person. We have written some professional success stories just by shifting a person from the wrong job into the right one.

The wisdom to make these decisions, often in dialogue with the employee and his or her peers, is one of the greatest challenges faced by the highest level of management in any organization – and it is one that we are continually striving to meet. At the same time, we work with our people to help them understand that a mid-career job shift need not be a signal of failure but rather a prelude to greater triumph.

Education in leadership is never fully completed. It's a lifetime project, part of the journey of self-discovery that never ends.

9

The mind knows no gender: the emerging promise of female leadership

We all realize that gender imbalance exists in the MENA region's work force. There are many initiatives aimed at addressing this issue by allowing society more flexibility in keeping with its values. We also know there is room to do more, and to do it with a difference. With Saudi Arabia and the MENA region being fully recognized and accepted as members of the global community, there is a greater need than ever before to provide equal opportunities for the human and economic advancement of both genders.

Female leadership is not alien to the region's culture. Throughout history, the region has been exemplified by outstanding women leaders who have entered the scene, excelled and made a lasting impression in the service of society. This tradition extends all the way back to Khadija bint Khuwaylid, who was the first and most beloved wife of the Prophet Muhammed (peace be upon him). Khadija inherited her father's business and managed it so successfully that her trading caravan was said to be by far the largest of all those in existence among the members of the Quraish tribe.

Today, women leaders in the region are continuing this tradition. When we see first-hand the talent and potential that exist today among the youth who represent prime candidates for enriching the leadership landscape in the region's institutions, this can only be the result of leadership in action on the part of both men and women. In short, it takes leaders to develop leaders.

At B.I.G., we believe that encouraging even greater achievement by promising women leaders is a pressing cause that touches all aspects of our society. Even with all of the media coverage, debate and attention given to this national topic, we as a society continue to fall short on delivery.

For over five decades, B.I.G. has consistently striven to be a responsible corporate citizen. Our deep-rooted appreciation for the value of talent and enterprise leadership led us to support the various national and regional efforts recognizing the role of women in the workplace. However, we wanted to do our part in a unique and unconventional way. The Achievers Award is one of the initiatives we've developed in pursuit of this goal.

By recognizing and paying tribute to women's leadership in the workplace, we hope to provide a route for women to 'set sail' and realize their full potential, as well as to act as effective mentors and role models for future women leaders. Our ultimate goal is that the Achievers Award, through a careful and even-handed selection process, will begin by recognizing qualified women leaders in Saudi Arabia and may eventually lead to the establishment of a private sector leadership academy for continuing education.

Our plan for the Achievers Award was approved by the B.I.G. board of directors, which has oversight of all the company's corporate social responsibility initiatives. Candidates for the award should be females with a college degree, a few years of work experience, and some other specific qualifications. We expect to present one prize to a leader from the business sector and another to a leader from either academia or the non-profit world. Most importantly, candidates should demonstrate in their life and work the leadership characteristics I discussed in detail in Chapter 4 of this book – that is, they should be able to show that they are visionary, authentic, nurturing, collaborative, resilient, and committed to excellence in execution.

You can learn more about the rules and procedures at the Achievers Award website, www.theachieversaward.com. Our aim is that, in 2013, the first year's award winners be selected.

The re-emergence of women as enterprise leaders

Our creation of the Achievers Award symbolizes B.I.G.'s commitment to encouraging young women in the region to develop their leadership skills to the fullest capacity. We believe this is crucial for the long-term success of Saudi Arabia and other countries in the Middle East. But of course we also recognize that, as with any significant cultural shift, promoting female leadership in the Middle East to a level of equality with male leadership will require many adjustments.

Some of these adjustments are on the personal level. Acceptance of women as colleagues, partners and leaders is not universal – especially, perhaps, for men who are unsure about their own leadership abilities. This is an issue that can only be addressed through effective leadership from the top and the gradual change of habits that increased familiarity usually brings.

When I see that some of my peers are having difficulty separating their personal attitudes about women from their relationships with female colleagues, I like to advise them: 'Listen with your mind, not your eyes!' In other words, rather than focusing on the fact that the person speaking happens to be female, pay attention to what she is saying! You are likely to discover that her words are worth listening to – and your assumptions about gender may begin to change as a result.

In some cases, regulations need to be changed to accommodate the needs and interests of women. Current laws and customs vary widely from one country to another. Some neighbouring regional countries are more encouraging for women in business than others. In many businesses, segregating women from men is a common practice. However, this marginalizes communication, and in today's world that is no longer a viable approach in most industries. We simply can't afford to miss the valuable input about our products, services, customers and practices that all of our workers have to provide – including workers of both genders.

Overall business policies and practices may also need to be adjusted. Some advocate the creation of a 'mothers' track' for women in business, where women with young children are given jobs with flexible schedules, work locations and travel requirements, so as to accommodate their needs as mothers. The practicality of this solution will vary by job and industry. Ambitious executives of both genders must be expected to deliver first-class results regardless of circumstances, but businesses need to find ways to adapt to the reality of women as mothers without losing the talents that they bring to the business world. We need to be ready to allow women to take time off from careers to raise their young children and then welcome them back to the work force without penalizing them unduly for their absence. Flexibility and open-mindedness will be keys to making these adjustments work fairly and productively for all.

On a personal level, I would urge young women who are wrestling with the challenge of balancing work and family life *not* to allow motherhood to completely derail their ambitions. If you are in this group, I would encourage you to stay involved in your work and career, even when your children are small and need a lot of care and attention. You may find it's practical to work part time, to serve as a consultant, or to organize your work from a home office. But remain engaged! Remember, the time will come when your children will get older, become more independent and eventually leave home. When that happens, you'll want something engrossing and meaningful to do – and your family may well need the income from a good job to help pay the bills. It's hard to start a new career from scratch, especially in the middle stages of your working life, so keep your career alive right through motherhood if you possibly can; you'll be glad you did.

Above all, attitudes need to change, on the part of everyone involved – including both men and women. All women need to learn to think of themselves as having serious long-term careers, something the female students I meet are just starting to embrace.

The attitude change we need is not only within businesses. Dr May Al-Dabbagh (whose connection with B.I.G. I'll discuss in detail a little later in this chapter) researched stress in the lives of working Saudi women for her PhD thesis at Oxford University. She conducted surveys and in-depth interviews with over 1,000 women working in a variety of fields in Saudi Arabia, from traditional areas like health care and education to other fields like business and finance. Her most consistent finding was that *non-work factors*, such as access to transport or child care, have a considerable effect on how women feel about their jobs. The take-home message? 'If Saudi Arabia wants to see more women in the work force', Dr May says, 'then national leaders need to look closely at non-work factors that affect job satisfaction, because women's ability to contribute successfully on the job is affected by a variety of factors that are not limited to the work domain.'

As you might imagine, the attitudes of husbands toward their wives' careers can also have a huge impact on the women involved.

Eventually, society must deal with the hidden issue – the readiness with which men unload the role of family caretaker exclusively onto women. If men can accept the notion that they, too, are responsible for bringing up their children, life will be better for aspiring women in Saudi society – and in the long run it will be better for families as well. Perhaps one day there will be a recognized 'fathers' track' for men who want to play a more active role in nurturing their off-spring, alongside the 'mothers' track'. I would encourage society to try such a social and business approach.

Too many people assume that family life and their careers are automatically in conflict with one another. When you make this assumption, a cycle is started whereby both sides of your existence are likely to suffer. I'm inclined to think that, in fact, family and career do not compete with one another but actually complement one another. Once you start to look at things from this perspective, the whole situation begins to improve.

DR MAY AL-DABBAGH
Step by step – the story of change

At B.I.G., we've found that driving the pace of change is a challenge in the arena of gender relations, as it is in any field where engaging with society at large is involved. Corporate training programmes will play an important role, but a culture shift of this magnitude is more than a training issue – it must be addressed by a serious commitment from the top of the organization. Timelines and objectives must be set and adhered to if the goal is real.

Managing these changes is a challenge we are currently immersed in at B.I.G. At the highest level, during 2011 we engaged our first female board member – Dr May Al-Dabbagh, a distinguished scholar with special expertise in gender issues, whose insights into the role of gender in work we've already quoted.

I'll never forget how I first heard of Dr May. Ever since my college days in the United States, I've devoted Sunday mornings to watching political talk shows from that country, such as *Meet the Press* and *Face the Nation*. One Sunday evening back home in Jeddah, I was flipping through the channels to get to my favourite shows when by chance I heard a Dubai channel that featured Dr May being interviewed about a symposium addressing more inclusive roles for women in the private sector. She was making a compelling point about the challenges women in the region face, the uneven playing field on which they must compete, and the light this conference would shed on the key issues for decision makers.

By the close of the interview, I was impressed by Dr May's perceptiveness, poise and thoughtfulness. The interviewer mentioned that she was associated with the Dubai School of Government, whose help we'd already been seeking regarding one of our corporate social responsibility initiatives. When I asked the director of the school for an opinion on Dr May as a candidate for our board position, he quickly assured me that Dr May would be an ideal choice. Others whose advice I sought were equally positive.

I proposed the position to Dr May, and, as I expected, she didn't just say 'I accept' immediately. Instead, she asked, 'Why me? After all, I am not a business person.'

I responded:

> *That's a fair question. Board effectiveness is critical to us, and we feel that having a woman with the right credentials can significantly improve the quality of our deliberations*

and the decisions we make. But business experience is
not what we're looking for. What we want is the right kind
of intellect and the ability to keep an eye on the bigger
picture – to bring a fresh perspective to the challenges
we face and the opportunities before us. Frankly, I
think that your academic background can only help us
address what you might call the software components of
our organization – the human issues that often make the
difference between success and failure.

To her credit, Dr May took time to think about the proposition and asked a number of other intelligent and thoughtful questions before deciding to accept the offer to join our board. Of course, she understood how unusual it was for a Saudi company with plans to go public some time in the future to offer a board seat to a woman, and I suspect this helped sway her decision. She knew that by taking on the challenge she would be playing a part in our efforts to change the corporate landscape of women's participation in decision-making positions in Saudi Arabia.

In the relatively brief time that Dr May has served with us, she has already contributed significantly to our understanding of some of the crucial management challenges we are facing – including those related to female empowerment. Her background, of course, is in the social sciences rather than business, but we've found that this divergent perspective has enabled Dr May to offer unique insights into the work we do.

For example, when our board was discussing plans for a new employment programme designed to enhance the 'localization' of our work force (that is, to attract and accommodate a higher percentage of Saudi nationals as opposed to foreign ex-pats), Dr May pointed out that students and other young people are often caught up in negative discourses about employment and likely to be particularly responsive to a programme that could help them tell a more positive story about localization and their experience with it. Since this is precisely the audience we hope to reach, we decided to call the pro-gramme STEP – an acronym for Saudization Talent Employment Program. This was an effective change in framing the issues at hand that Dr May's personal connection with the student population enabled her to propose.

In other cases, Dr May's non-traditional orientation allows her to 'think outside the box' when the board is evaluating business opportunities. On more than one occasion in the midst of a debate between alternatives – neither of them ideal – Dr May has spoken up to ask: 'Have we really exhausted all the possible options? Can you trace for me the decision process that has led us to this point?' With her scholarly insights into how social structures can shape – and often restrict – the possibilities that people perceive, Dr May has exhibited to the board how a wider net can be cast, inviting potential breakthrough ideas that come from outside the usual channels.

Dr May Al-Dabbagh exemplifies the qualities of an Unknown Leader. Armed simply with the gumption she has developed from years of study and reflection, she is able to help those around her embrace new ways of thinking that break down barriers, create opportunities and solve intractable problems. When full equality is enjoyed by women everywhere, credit will be partly due to women like Dr May, working quietly and effectively behind the scenes in thousands of workplaces around the world.

Opening doors to invite change

At B.I.G., we are also working to increase female representation at other levels in the company. One opportunity is in our new flavours business, which produces flavours for use in food products of all sorts, mostly based on natural extracts and all produced to the high-est standards of quality and purity. It's a joint venture that we've launched in partnership with MANE SA, a highly respected French company that has been in the flavourings business since 1871. Banawi

MANE Flavors, or, as we brand it, Lazeez, has employed as its first 'flavourist in the making' a young Saudi woman recently graduated from college with a degree in biochemistry.

Elsewhere at B.I.G., the relative presence of women workers varies according to historical, cultural and local factors. We are a manufacturing company in the business-to-business arena, a sector in which women have traditionally been under-represented. (Their presence is relatively greater in service companies and in consumer products markets.) Nevertheless some divisions of B.I.G. already have a notable female presence. In our Egyptian operations, for example, women make up close to a third of our total employee base. We appointed a woman as head of our research lab in Cairo at the start of our business there. In other divisions, the percentage of women employees is smaller, but it is growing, and we are determined to continue increasing it to get closer and closer to parity, depending, of course, on the availability of women with the specific skills and knowledge required to drive our future success. Thankfully, the growing number of young women graduating from top universities in the MENA region and elsewhere offers an increasing supply of the female business talent we will need to achieve our goals in the years to come.

We're pursuing these objectives with what I might call 'deliberate speed' – pressing forward on a change agenda driven by a clear vision of a more inclusive business environment, while also being careful to manage the psychological, social and leadership adjustments that need to be made. Rushing into change without laying a firm foundation in the hearts and minds of people can be a recipe for disaster.

Dr May has been very supportive of this approach. As she observes:

> *Successful change includes appointing competent women,*
> *but it also includes transforming the system itself.*
> *Limiting efforts to token appointments could be a setback*
> *to a long-term programme of change because it will give us*

all an illusory sense of direction. I think it is commendable that B.I.G. is aiming to achieve a few unequivocal gains. This will allow those pioneering women to serve as ambassadors to represent our new approach and to attract others like them.

That's exactly the plan we are now following.

Looking at the experiences of our friends in North America and Europe, we know that issues surrounding gender relationships can be complicated even in societies where men and women have inter-acted on a more equal footing for decades. Witness, for example, the controversies over accusations of sexual harassment sometimes levelled at Western business executives.

Cases like these remind us that the road to change can be bumpy, even when the eventual goal is one that everyone agrees upon and that is long overdue. We're taking care to map out our course toward a more accommodating future with thoughtful diligence, so that the transition can be as trouble-free as possible. Our human resources professionals have a major responsibility in this area, and they are handling the challenge with enormous dedication and skill. And it's worth noting that our current corporate head of recruitment is a woman – a further indication of our serious commitment to giving women meaningful leadership roles in the growth of B.I.G.

Social influences and the growth of female employment

Change regarding something as fundamental as gender expectations can be surprisingly complicated to achieve. Cause-and-effect relation-ships among social, economic, political and psychological factors can be very complicated, difficult to untangle and even harder to change.

Consider, as a single small example, the use of social media like Facebook, Twitter and YouTube among women in the Arab world. It's a topic of great interest among social scientists, since these media have become some of the most powerful agents of change and social cohesion in the contemporary world. It also happens to be one of the subjects that Dr May has focused on in a recent report published by the Gender and Public Policy Programme she runs.

According to the report, male and female respondents indicated that they view social media as an effective tool for women's empowerment. However, a 'virtual' gender gap prevails, as only one third of Facebook users in the Arab region are women. By contrast, around the world, women are about half of Facebook users. What explains the difference?

The report highlighted the fact that environmental factors constitute the largest barriers to Arab women's use of social media, specifically 'societal and cultural constraints', in addition to 'access to ICT'. These factors help to shape the environment in which female social media users operate. Personal factors, which have more to do with the skills and abilities of female social media users themselves, such as 'levels of education' or 'ICT literacy' for example, were also listed as barriers, but were less significant than the environmental factors.

So how can this 'virtual' gender gap be closed? If the barriers to gender equality in social media use were mainly personal, then any interventions to address this gender gap should be focused on 'fixing the women', so to speak – for example, by introducing more training for women or increasing their education. However, the regional survey results clearly showed that barriers are predominantly environmental and require efforts to address gender-biased attitudes, cultural constraints and discriminatory allocation of resources and opportunities.

What's the value of research like this? Among other things, it can help those who hope to be change agents to determine what sorts of social interventions are likely to be effective in promoting greater gender equality.

Making full use of the 50 per cent of our human capital that wears a female face represents a major social shift. It will take time and a willingness to learn and change on the part of every sector of society. It makes sense to have business, academia and government working together to encourage this change, and to make sure that it happens in a way that strengthens and enhances the social bonds that unite society rather than damaging them.

The one thing I don't worry about is finding bright young women to become part of the next generation of leaders for the MENA region. I've met many who have all the makings of tomorrow's leaders. The challenge lies in creating new opportunities for them to learn, grow and develop in a nurturing environment – but this is a challenge I'm confident we will meet.

10

The challenge of the Arab Spring: toward a vibrant, entrepreneurial Middle East

The regional youth movement now called the Arab Spring began on 17 December 2010 with a single tragic event. A 26-year-old Tunisian street vendor named Mohamed Bouazizi set himself on fire to protest about his treatment at the hands of a local government official. Bouazizi's act became a catalyst for demonstrations throughout the country, which grew especially heated after his death on 4 January 2011. Within days, the country's president had been forced to step down after 23 years in power. The Tunisian revolution proved to be the first of a cascading series of upheavals that have affected over a dozen countries and led to regime changes in several of them. In recognition of the symbolic power of Bouazizi's act, the respected newspaper *The Times* of London named him Person of the Year for 2011.

The long-term effects of the Arab Spring are still playing out, and it's not yet clear what the final blend of positive and negative impacts will be, but I think it is significant to note that Bouazizi's suicide was driven not so much by political motives as by economic ones. Bouazizi was not a pro-democracy activist or freedom fighter. He was an aspiring entrepreneur whose grandest dream was to save enough money to buy a pickup truck to bring his goods to market. It was frustration with the government red tape that led to the confiscation of his unlicensed vegetable cart that finally drove Bouazizi to his act of self-destructive violence.

My point is that the Arab Spring is *not* just about politics. It is not just a matter of voting rights, freedom of speech, the right to organize political parties, and so on – important as these are. It is also about opening up the economy so that more people will be able to participate more fully and freely, creating better futures for themselves and their families even as they build their communities, their countries and the entire region.

If you seek a barometer to measure the aspirations of youth in a given society, ask a cross-section of young people what they dream about achieving in their careers and in their lives. If many or most talk about just making ends meet, one day at a time, and speak as if overcoming even a small hurdle is a significant accomplishment, you are looking at a society where the unrealized potential of youth is in danger of evaporating, unfulfilled, as the years unfold.

Today, the Arab Spring is just one symptom of the epochal changes we are now living through – in the world as a whole, and specifically in the Middle East.

Change is inevitable, including change that touches individuals' personal choices and aspirations for a better life and a bigger say in influencing the shape and future of their communities and societies. This fact is indisputable in historical terms, even though at times it may seem to be merely wishful thinking.

So if we believe that time is on the side of those who yearn for change, then it's fair to say that those who defend inertia and hold on to the status quo are on the wrong side of history. But how can we, as individuals and as a society, trigger and pursue the right mode of change? And how can leadership in the Middle East address, navigate and manage change for us all?

Recent events in the region speak volumes in response to these questions. These are questions all of us must grapple with, and which I confront daily as both a citizen of this region and an instigator of corporate change within B.I.G. While corporate change is not in the same league as national or regional change, there are some similarities. A leader's ultimate mandate is to visualize positive change, articulate it, and initiate the entire process so that society as a whole owns it and directs it towards a satisfying fruition. If we as society are not willing to adopt and embrace positive change – if we prefer to cling to inertia and the status quo – then we don't need leaders! Mere administrators – jugglers of complex systems and processes – will do just fine.

But here is where the dilemma lies: if leaders don't have their hand on the pulse of the people, if they fail to comprehend the aspirations of those they lead, they are likely to direct the nation or the enterprise to a much slower pace of change, one that may ultimately lead to a loss of momentum and a return of the inertia they'd sought to overcome in the first place.

When this happens, the leaders start looking back while the people are looking ahead. The leaders proudly declare, 'Look how far we have come!' while the people lament, 'Look how far behind we are!' And over time the gap between those who govern and those who are governed grows larger and larger.

If there is one thing we now know for certain, it is that recent events have catalysed the unifying energy of the youth of the MENA region in unprecedented ways that are rewriting history. The region's young men and women have dreams and aspirations just like those of their peers anywhere else in the world. That wasn't the case in previous generations. The digital age and its continual, instantaneous communication have globally linked individuals' dreams, aspirations, expectations and needs to a greater degree than ever before. As a result, the region's youth now expect similar agendas for prosperity from their leaders and governments to those expected by their peers around the world, along with a greater degree of accountability from their leaders.

In the face of this monumental shift in goals and expectations, leadership cannot afford to try to hold back the giant wave of energy from people demanding to be heard and taken seriously. But if leadership does embrace the vision of a society where change is a way of life, then leadership must manage that change and navigate us through it, steering us toward positive forms of change and away from the dangers of chaos, disorder or despair. The goal must be an enhanced quality of life that balances people's desire for a greater say in their future with a renewed commitment to a civil society and national values that bring us all together – one people, one nation, one destiny.

I believe the Arab Spring is also about achieving greater transparency in the public service arena and a greater sense of accountability to the people; and about instituting due process in governance that affects the daily lives of ordinary men and women and also in the equitable use of our national resources.

Although the phrase 'Arab Spring' has become a familiar one, I want to caution against exaggerated expectations concerning the pace of national and regional transformation. I hope that today's changes will ultimately lead to an enhanced process of nation building for the entire Middle East. That will require patience and resolve from all of us. We must look forward to a natural political process that extends through all four seasons of the year – not just a hopeful spring.

In this final chapter, I want to address and try to describe some of the challenges this new era presents to us, and describe the critical role tomorrow's leaders must play in helping us meet those challenges. And make no mistake, leadership is the resource of which we are in most dire need. In the words of my friend Nabil Alyousuf, 'There's no shortage of funds or ideas. The shortage is people who can actually get things done and execute' – in a word, leaders.

In a world that is transforming, we as individuals must also transform ourselves. That's the message at the core of this book. If each of us develops his or her leadership capabilities to the fullest degree possible, our societies will also be better equipped to tackle the enormous economic, political and social challenges they face in the 21st century. To help make this possible, our societies must simultaneously evolve to make sure that every young person has the greatest possible opportunity to exercise his or her God-given talents for the benefit of all.

Is it too early to prepare for a post-petroleum world?

Perhaps the greatest single challenge we face in the MENA region is developing a long-term plan for dealing with the mixed blessing of oil wealth. The sudden discovery of this 'black gold' in the early years of the last century leapfrogged the Gulf region from a pre-industrial state into being one of the richest and most influential regions of the world. Yet the genie of oil has proven to be a double-edged sword. Although plenty has been accomplished so far by relying on the wealth created by petroleum, we have not yet done enough to turn this wealth into broader, sustainable prosperity for the entire society. Furthermore, the riches produced by oil will run out eventually, or be rendered obsolete by issues of climate change, environmental degradation and renewable energy sources.

We have also built political alliances with nations that are major customers for the oil we produce, which means that our international relations tend to shift as the oil trade shifts. This kind of entanglement between politics and business is natural, but we are still learning to manage it effectively for the long-term benefit of our society. We need to separate the two so that we can perform our proper role as players on the world stage with many diverse interests.

More broadly, it is time for us to prepare for a post-petroleum world – to define what such a world looks like and envision plans for getting there. Leaders for the MENA region must articulate a vision of hope for the future that will inspire and mobilize the energies of the young people, too many of whom now feel disengaged and indifferent. Some of the best and brightest are already leaving the region, eventually leading to a brain drain that is undermining our future prospects. At the same time that we work to make the region more enticing as a long-term home for the most talented youth, we need to do a better job of assimilating the diverse pool of highly specialized skills and crafts of foreign nationals who come to the region to work. Other societies have learned to benefit from the social, ethnic and cultural diversity that globalization brings. The Middle East needs to do the same within the particular nuances of our national cultures.

Making the best of diversity is not a simple matter. On the one hand, diversity is not an option – it is a present reality. In my country of Saudi Arabia and in our region as a whole, we already have significant diversity. Every company, every business and every social institution in our society has it. To a large and increasing extent, we are already making use of the talents of people from varied backgrounds to help grow our economies and our nations, and this is a positive thing.

However, at the same time, there continues to be some resistance to the need to acknowledge and accept diversity, and to find ways of integrating those committed people of diverse foreign backgrounds into our social fabric. While many of our young people have been exposed to a diversified classroom environment and academic environment, others have not, and as a result they may feel uneasy being part of a new global world. In business, we often hire foreign nationals to fill critical positions, while at the same time we impose pressure on ourselves to give preference to local workers. Do we fully accept those among us who come from foreign backgrounds as part of our developing nationhood? Would our future be better served by allowing those with special skills and crafts within our diverse visiting workforce to assimilate as part of our developing nationhood? Are we willing to accept diversity in our classrooms, workplaces, sports arenas and cultural venues as an integral part of our society that will make us better suited for the competitive global landscape? The answers to those questions are not yet clear.

There is no perfect solution to this dilemma, as the experience of other countries shows. The United States and, in more recent history, a few European countries have done a better job than most of embracing diversity while pursuing a clearly defined national agenda. But even in Western societies, stresses exist between the desire of ethnic communities to maintain their traditions and the desire to create and maintain a unified sense of national identity. It's not surprising that the peoples of our region are grappling with some of the same conflicts. This is a serious challenge that deserves to be high on our national agenda in the years to come.

Building the civic sector towards a more inclusive society

One way to address the 'engagement gap' among many of the region's young people is for us deliberately to nurture civic institutions that can engage all the people, encourage debate, and present alternative ideas about the future. The civic sector we need to encourage may include educational institutions, news media, forums for exchange of ideas, think tanks, non-profit organizations devoted to diverse social causes, and so on. Much of the dynamism of Western societies is based on the existence of a vibrant 'third sector' of this sort, and the MENA region would benefit from a similar network of institutions.

My experience is chiefly with the business community within our region, where I've observed that the relative weakness of the civic sector sometimes makes it harder for society to address economic and business-related issues holistically and effectively. For example, we have not instituted an effective formal body that serves as a conduit for concerns, interests and ideas from business leaders to those in government. Since the 1990s, a number of countries in the Gulf region have had consultative councils or national assemblies with members who are appointed by and answerable to the head of state. These are useful bodies that have the right to propose legislation to the head of state, but because of their limited charters and their closed-end structure they are hard for ordinary citizens like business leaders to use as forums for their concerns. The Chambers of Commerce and Industry provide a venue for a certain level of free discussion of business issues, but they seem like 'orphans' without any formal role in the policy formation structure.

Thus there's no real counterpart in the regional system to the many think tanks, lobbying organizations and industry associations in other societies that are continually proposing new programmes for public discussion and legislative debate, or to public events like legislative meetings where ordinary citizens who equitably and fairly represent the various constituencies of society have an opportunity directly to address lawmakers with their concerns and suggestions and influence the legislative agenda. As a result of this gap, there's no clear structured way for important new ideas or growing problems to translate into policy reviews, fact-finding studies and legislative proposals, finally emerging as effective new laws, policies, and public policy directions.

Lack of a vibrant civic sector in the region means a kind of missing link in the structure of society. Over time, I hope this will change.

We also have an obligation to allocate national funds to educate and train legislators-to-be. If we jump too fast into the transformational stage of bringing unprepared citizens into the legislative arena, we run the risk of introducing lawmakers that are not ready for proper legislation. Thus, there is urgency to fast-track the process of indoctrinating aspiring legislators, but we must not do this at the expense of proper governance and quality. Moving too early will short-change our transformational process and the value of national debate, law-making and our legislative *modus operandi*.

Dr Haifa Al-Lail, president of Effat University, has made development of a richer, more lively civic sector a personal cause. She believes that the lack of such a sector is due, in part, to legal impediments:

> *Right now, although we have foundations and NGOs*
> *that operate effectively in Saudi Arabia, we still miss*
> *a governance umbrella to provide systematic oversight,*
> *regulate their incorporation, and encourage their growth.*
> *This means that NGOs don't have clear guidance as to how*
> *they are supposed to operate and what their rights and*
> *responsibilities are. Islamic principles and laws provide*
> *a potentially solid foundation for the civic sector, but we*
> *have not yet done enough to build on these principles.*

According to Dr Haifa, the venerable Islamic tradition of charity needs to be expanded to include support for civic sector organizations:

> *Charity is fine, but we need to develop the custom of*
> *giving not only to poor people but also to institutions to*
> *establish schools, hospitals, clinics, training programmes*
> *for the unemployed, and similar service centres. Lacking*
> *this tradition, people are not aware of what we mean by*
> *giving to institutions to establish themselves, so they give*
> *to individuals instead. And they give generously and*

repeatedly, but they don't think that giving to institutions really matters, because they assume that the government has this responsibility.

Government can do plenty to encourage individuals and organizations to donate generously to NGOs through incentives and expense deductions. But Dr Haifa's comments about the Islamic tradition of charity suggest the possibility that the relative weakness of our civic sector may have long-standing cultural roots. People in the region may tend to assume that any matter that is *not* under the control of the central government is, therefore, purely in the hands of private citizens, whether business people, families or individuals. The idea that a third sector of institutions might exist that is independent of the state yet helps to address major social problems by organizing, motivating, educating and channelling the energies of millions of citizens is still a somewhat unfamiliar one. A concerted effort to enhance the role of the civic sector will help to change this cultural pattern in a way that can benefit the region's societies enormously.

Work and self-esteem: two sides of a coin

Right now, unemployment is another of the major challenges of the MENA region. This is particularly the case among young people, where the unemployment rate may run in some countries upwards of 20 per cent. Given the fact that populations in the MENA region are heavily weighted toward youth, this means we have tens of millions of young people without enough work to keep them busy, productive and engaged. It's a formula for dissatisfaction, alienation and long-term economic stagnation. Work is not just a source of income (important as that is). It's also a source of self-esteem, a way for individuals to contribute to their society, and an opportunity for people to develop the personal vision that gives meaning to life. Without enough useful work to do, we regress, both as individuals and as a society.

Unemployment is one of the chief reasons for the eruption of the Arab Spring in 2011. Mohamed Bouazizi was just one of millions of young people suffering because of lack of economic opportunity. The demonstrations were, in part, a cry for help on the part of the young people: 'Give us work that we can believe in and that will call forth our best efforts in a worthy cause!' It's up to our societies to respond to this heartfelt call.

Thankfully, most countries in the MENA region continue to have strong family structures. These provide an informal 'safety net' that protects young people from the worst economic effects of unemployment. Rather than having thousands of out-of-work young people jostling for places to sleep in government- or charity-run shelters – or, even worse, on city streets or in shanty towns – many have moved back in with their parents, aunts and uncles, or other relatives. It's much better than nothing, but no one sees this as a permanent solution. The need for economic growth to help young people find jobs and be able to build homes and families of their own is critical.

Governments have a major role to play in dealing with the unemployment problem, especially in the short term. Public sector work programmes can help to fill the gap between high school or college graduation and a long-term career in the private sector, so that millions of young people don't find themselves idle and losing the habits of work and self-discipline that make such a difference to lifelong success.

However, a lot depends on the *kind* of jobs we create in the public sector. If we invest in necessary infrastructure projects – roads, bridges, rails, tunnels, seaports, airports, pipelines, the electrical grid, schools, universities, hospitals and so on – we will provide constructive employment to thousands of young workers, including architects, engineers, electricians, plumbers, landscape artists and many other kinds of employees. At the same time, we will be building projects of long-term value for society, many of which will contribute to future economic growth.

During the Great Depression of the 1930s, the US government under President Franklin D. Roosevelt hired hundreds of thousands of young people to build highways, bridges, dams, schoolhouses and libraries, and to enhance the natural beauty of the country by creating national parks, forest reserves and wilderness areas. These infrastructure projects helped fuel the nation's economic growth and improve the citizens' quality of life for decades afterwards. We can create similar programmes in the countries of the MENA region today.

Tackling unemployment through short-term infrastructure projects can be more than worthwhile. On the other hand, if we try to solve the unemployment dilemma by creating long-term jobs in the government bureaucracy, the solution may be worse than the problem! These jobs are not economically sustainable, because they don't create the most efficient forms of new wealth for ordinary individuals and families – unlike, for example, airports, highways and schools, all of which improve the country's capacity for productive enterprise. By contrast, newly-created bureaucratic jobs only produce a drag on the economy, siphoning money into agencies that may produce unnecessary regulations, generate paperwork and otherwise add more complexities to everyday life for those in the private arena. Government officials who want to address the problem of youth unemployment need to be very careful about *how* they go about it. One path can be productive and sustainable; the other can be just the opposite.

Governments can also help reduce unemployment through programmes other than direct employment. One example is an innovative government-sponsored project in my home country of Saudi Arabia that my friend Hani Khoja, founder of the consulting firm Elixir, is helping to lead.

'Unemployment is a huge issue in Saudi Arabia', Hani says. 'We've got to create tens of thousands of jobs a year just to keep the unemployment rate from rising.' In response, Elixir has helped to create a multi-pronged programme that is using modern marketing techniques to bring more young Saudi citizens into the work force. Elixir's challenge is to change mindsets – to convince those who do the hiring that the negative stereotypes some of them believe about unemployed Saudis are wrong. The programme includes publicizing stories about companies that have achieved success by hiring local workers, creating opportunities for company leaders who have hired Saudi employees to share their experiences with one another, and offering advice about how small adjustments to organizational design or human resources strategies can help make it easier to bring local employees on board and to do so successfully – and profitably.

Of course, changing attitudes across a large swathe of society is easier said than done – even when the national government is sponsoring the initiative. 'It's a real leadership challenge, trying to reverse 30 years' worth of thinking that has become deeply embedded in our culture', Hani says. 'But one element of a leader's job is to set forth a vision of where you want to be. Maybe that vision already exists in part; maybe it isn't as widespread as you want it to be, but you've got to believe that it will eventually become real.'

Elixir is using every tool at its disposal, from television and newspapers to social media, to promote an idealistic vision of the Saudi economy of the future: a meritocracy in which hard work is both necessary and rewarded; a world in which all kinds of employment are respected; and a world in which men and women with skill, creativity, drive and energy can find excitement and satisfaction in building businesses, wealth and long-term prosperity for the nation and the region.

The Elixir programme to change Saudi attitudes about work and careers is just a partial answer to the challenge of unemployment, but it illustrates one of the important roles that government can play. When a society needs to make a cultural adjustment in order to be better equipped for the future, government can use its unmatched power to communicate with its citizens to promote a positive vision of change and the benefits it promises.

Notice, too, that the Elixir programme is an example of 'soft power' in the hands of government – persuasion and attitude change – rather than the 'hard power' of strict regulation and penalties. In recent years, there has been controversy over national laws requiring 'Saudization' or 'localization' of specified proportions of a company's work force. These laws are well-intentioned attempts to make companies hire local workers rather than relying on foreigners, but I'm concerned that they can sometimes hamstring businesses and limit their flexibility unduly. I think that, in the long run, government can do more to address the unemployment issue through programmes of education, retraining and cultural uplift than through the heavy hand of regulation.

Society as a whole benefits from a healthy employment record just as much as the individual. However, as we've all seen, government-funded unemployment benefit programmes, while often justified and necessary, place a heavy fiscal burden on a country. The problem increases when a country has an expansive youth population with varying levels of education.

I've always subscribed to the school of thought that says that sustainable employment cannot be realized through force or authority, but through continual engagement between public and private enterprise. This allows private businesses to view government not as a stick but as an enabler, while also allowing government to work with businesses in various sectors towards advancing the hiring of more citizens and improving their skill levels. Each business sector and subsector should have appropriate representation at the department of labour to allow for this reciprocal engagement, starting with open dialogue, one to one and in groups, leading to joint plans to hire more locals, cooperative site visits to monitor results, continual reviews, and adjustments as necessary.

This approach may sound complex and time-consuming. Maybe so. But I've never seen the heavy hand of power alone lead to a sustainable solution to a long-term social or cultural imbalance. Private sector employment is a much more productive machine than any government mandate for absorbing the countless numbers of un-employed youth. In addition, private sector employment allows for high-skilled jobs to be created and funded. This leads, in turn, to an increase in per capita income and purchasing power as well as the self-esteem that can come only from a decent job that provides fair pay and personal achievement.

With these goals in mind, let us work together, public and private, to create a climate of partnership to achieve the sustainable employ-ment we all need and must have as a society.

Creating the spark for an entrepreneurial economy

Over time, we will also need to rethink the basis of the region's economy. The oil supplies that produce so much of the wealth today will not last for ever. And over time – although it may take decades – the oil reserves will dwindle, driving the market price higher, making alternative energy sources, including renewables like wind, solar and others, more attractive. Concerns about global climate change will further encourage a gradual reduction in the world's reliance on petroleum.

The challenge, then, is for the countries in the region to build a more diverse industrial and business base that will provide inter-esting, well-paid jobs for a large number of people. This will lead to broader distribution of wealth, which in turn will produce an even stronger economy, as an increasingly large and prosperous working class and middle class will be able to improve their quality of life and so promote long-term growth.

To support this kind of economic development, we need to make sure that regulations, customs, laws and habits of thinking are all evolving to promote entrepreneurship and bottom-up development. Entrepreneurs are the engine of growth in any society – the creators of innovation, sustainable employment, wealth and opportunity. To slow, weaken or divert that engine is very alarming.

Some people mistakenly believe that entrepreneurship and even the very spirit of capitalism are somehow in conflict with Islam or with the innate culture of the Muslim world. This is false. I've already spoken about the merchant culture of the region, which has an ancient history dating back many centuries. Arab dedication to commerce can be traced back to the caravan routes that once connected the Far East with Europe, along which a string of great trading cities grew up – Istanbul, Damascus, Baghdad, Mecca, Sana'a.

And if the issue is Islam, I might point out that it is the only one of the world's great religions whose messenger was a merchant! The social and economic principles of Islam were specifically designed to encourage trade. The only cost imposed on business people by Islam was the famous *zakat*, a form of tax (usually at the rate of 2.5 per cent) whose proceeds are designated for the relief of the poor.

The reality is that entrepreneurship is second nature to people in the MENA region – part of the DNA. Unfortunately, excessive involvement in the economy by well-intentioned government officials in many countries of the region has had a stifling effect on our natural entrepreneurial spirit. The historical reasons for this phenomenon are not difficult to understand. The oil riches that have shaped the region's development for most of the last century are mostly under the control and stewardship of national governments. The fact that the governments are the custodians of the region's natural resources is indisputable, but economic policy development must include private sector leadership. Otherwise economic policies, priorities and expectations can fall short of achieving the growth parameters needed. Managing oil wealth understandably takes centre stage, but it shouldn't be at the expense of creating the right economic conditions for independent businesses to flourish.

As I've observed, the era of oil will not last forever. Even today we are seeing evidence of the fact that oil alone can't create the opportunities for meaningful work and self-development that young people naturally crave. We need to develop dynamic economies to get more done with less and unleash the creativity waiting to find expression in the lives of millions of young people in the region. Finally, we need to ensure efficient access to capital for creative business minds, including small companies that may have the seeds of enormous growth for the future.

Shifting to this entrepreneurial model of economic growth will require a leap of faith on the part of everyone in the region. Entrepreneurship is a bottom-up phenomenon driven by individual creativity, not by central planning platforms, which tend to derail national development as countries in the region expand in population and complexity. That means that no one can completely control the nature, direction or speed of entrepreneurial development – whether they are industrial leaders, financial executives or government officials. We need to have faith in the energy, creativity and intelligence of the region's people and make certain they have the tools and the opportunities they need to produce tomorrow's breakthroughs. Entrepreneurs don't need handouts; they are naturally prone to navigate tough terrains and survive, even prosper. But they need the right climate to generate economic growth.

In concrete terms, this means we need to be willing to restrain the tendency to over-regulate businesses – to make would-be entrepreneurs run through gauntlets of regulations, licences, certificates, fees, tariffs and documentation before they can start creating wealth. Unless a deliberate effort at restraint is made, regulations have a natural tendency to multiply and accumulate, sometimes without even being noticed. A perceived problem gives rise to a new government office, which issues a set of new rules, which require yet another series of forms and approvals. Eventually, the burden becomes so great that countless people give up on starting their own businesses, depriving the community of the benefits of their talents, and depriving the economy of needed growth.

Furthermore, in today's climate, managing and developing a small business can easily become a source of worry for an entrepreneur because of over-regulation. As a result, entrepreneurs may opt to keep their businesses as they are rather than strive to expand them, satisfied simply to sustain their current relatively comfortable lifestyle and forgo the challenge of growth. This is a tragic outcome – not so much for individual entrepreneurs as for society. When entrepreneurs develop their businesses, the direct benefits they enjoy do not compare to the greater benefits they bring to society in the form of additional jobs and opportunities for young people to create new wealth.

Over-regulation generates other costs to society. It slows the process of innovation by creating barriers to speedy business development, ultimately leading to an environment in which companies tend to be one or two beats behind their competitors from other regions. This excessive red tape imposes a kind of 'invisible tax' on business activities, forcing companies to hire extra staff just to deal with paperwork, and thereby reducing profitability across the board. It creates temptations for under-the-table dealings and the emergence of illicit businesses that short-circuit the system.

Remember, too, that we are living in an increasingly globalized business environment. Legal, technological and economic barriers between countries and regions are being removed. If a particular country or region is plagued by over-regulation, it's relatively easy for the would-be entrepreneur to decamp to another location, even another continent, where a more business friendly environment has been established. Over-regulation is like a heavy weight that drags down the momentum for growth and prosperity, severely handicapping a country in the competitive race in the international arena.

Finally, because regulations in one country are inconsistent with those in neighbouring countries, experience in dealing with one bureaucratic system is not transferable to the next (unlike other forms of business knowledge). The business person dealing with governmental red tape must start the process from scratch in each new country, which represents a major hurdle to intra-regional investment and development. If we want to encourage regional growth, we need to simplify and unify the regulatory processes, which will make it easy for great businesses to spread and expand not just in one or two countries but across the entire region.

Here is a modest suggestion for reversing the natural tendency toward over-regulation: Let's require government agencies to quantify the economic cost, tangible and intangible, of any new regulation before it is promulgated. If the cost is greater than the expected benefit, the proposed regulation should be shelved. Adherence to this rule would slow the proliferation of unnecessary regulations. The next step would be to begin applying the same analysis to exist-ing regulations, one by one – and to eliminate those steps and stops whose costs outweigh the benefits. Over time, this would lead to a healthy pruning of outdated, needless rules, a drastic simplification of the bureaucracy and the regulatory system, and a vast freeing up of entrepreneurial energies. (It would also free up government employees to spend more time in productive services that benefit all the people of the nation.)

When entrepreneurship is stifled, its spark goes dim and the economy is stagnant, one common response is to call for govern-ment intervention to stimulate the economy – often through cen-trally planned programmes of industry building and employment. Unfortunately, this too often leads to a dead end. In the long run, only private sector employment holds real promise for the millions of talented, energetic, yet underemployed young people. Fortun-ately, there are entrepreneurs in the region who understand this and are eager to expand the opportunities for young workers by building new businesses or enlarging existing ones to employ them. What's more, some of these entrepreneurs recognize that the 'problem' of the huge youth population also represents a giant opportunity.

For example, my friend Nabil Alyousuf, whose work on behalf of the Dubai government I described in Chapter 2, is now working in the private sector as an investor who identifies and supports new businesses with exciting prospects for long-term growth. Nabil looks at the demographics of the MENA region and sees them as rich with opportunity:

> *Fifty per cent of the population of our region is less than 25 years old. It's a growing population with specific needs and interests. These millions of young people need education. They need health care. And they are eager to be connected with the world through technology, as we see through the phenomenal growth of internet penetration in our region. The young people who are using the internet now – boys and girls who are 15 or 16 years old – will grow in the next few years to become a huge market for information products and services. And in all of these areas there is a big gap to be filled – in education, in health care and in information services.*

> *At the same time, you see that governments are stretched when it comes to providing health care, education, and information and internet services. This creates opportunities for the private sector. For this reason, my investment company is focusing on education, health care, and information services as targets for growth. For example, we're investing in an electronic education platform being designed specifically for the Arab world. We're backing a health insurance company that is already operating successfully in the Emirates and has plans to expand into Saudi Arabia.*

> *Even unemployment among young people creates internet business opportunities. For instance, we see that there is a major difference between the wages in the Gulf and in other countries like Egypt and the Levant. So we're working*

with an entrepreneur in Egypt to create an outsourcing website so that small- to medium-size companies in the Emirates can get jobs done by young workers sitting in their homes in Lebanon and Syria. The companies win by getting talented but affordable employees, and the young workers win by getting productive work to do that boosts their skills and generates income for their families.

Entrepreneurs like Nabil Alyousuf, Ghazi Binzagr, Asma Siddiki, Moataz Al-Afi, Hani Khoja and other creative business leaders represent the best long-term solution to the youth unemployment problem in the region. Growing private sector companies hire workers, buy goods and services from supplier companies, create wealth, and fuel further growth throughout local and regional economies. They represent the hope for our future, and for the future of millions of young people in search of interesting, challenging, engaging work to do. By far the most powerful step that government can take in this area is to create a low-regulation environment in which business people can flourish. Simply getting government to ease its grip on the private sector will do a lot to promote individual creativity, economic growth and wealth creation that will benefit the entire society.

Fresh funds and entrepreneurial ventures: the inseparable bond between lungs and oxygen

Lack of access to investment capital is one of the many obstacles that new entrepreneurs must overcome in pursuit of their business dreams, and reducing this barrier would be one positive role that government can play in encouraging entrepreneurship. For example, it can support the creation and funding of local, national or regional economic development banks, specifically dedicated to lending money to small and medium-sized businesses (SMEs). Government could also require existing commercial banks to make credit available to SMEs, perhaps through a programme of government-backed loan guarantees. (In the United States, the Small Business Administration offers a service like this, and similar programmes exist in other countries.)

In the short term, until solutions like these are implemented, individual entrepreneurs must use their own ingenuity and creativity to find resources. It's a challenge that is particularly acute for female entrepreneurs – not just in the MENA region, but around the world. Because women have traditionally played a smaller role in public and business life than men, they often don't have access to the personal networks men have. They may also lack the track records of personal and business success that institutions like banks look to when evaluating an individual's creditworthiness. This handicap prevents many women from even reaching the starting line in the race for entrepreneurial success.

If you are an aspiring entrepreneur, male or female, I would offer a few simple suggestions for overcoming these and other barriers. In many cases, it will be more practical to rely on individuals rather than institutions as sources of start-up funds. This means networking as widely as possible. Don't speak only to family members and close friends; ask them to connect you with their friends, and with friends of friends. You think you are part of a very small community until you start asking for help – at which point you may discover that the network to which you belong is surprisingly large.

It's important to engage potential business sponsors on a professional basis. For the purposes of this conversation, you are not speaking to an uncle, an aunt or a friend; you are addressing a possible business partner, whom you should treat just as you would a banker or financier whom you are approaching with a proposal. Write up a concise business plan describing your concept, the funds required, the structure of the business and how you expect to make a profit. (There are books and websites offering specific guidance on crafting such a plan.) Do your homework – make sure you know everything there is to know about the business you want to create, the market in which you will compete, the costs of the products or services you will offer, the potential risks you anticipate and above all the niche you will serve and the value proposition you will offer. Put on the table a clear proposal to your prospective sponsor. If you want to borrow a certain sum, suggest a specific time frame for repayment. If you want to offer a share in the ownership of your business, be prepared to explain when you expect to be profitable and how much income you expect the business to generate for your investors over time.

The more diligent you are in thinking through your proposal, the more effectively you'll be able to present it. This is a great opportunity to further hone your communication skills. Develop what's called an 'elevator pitch' to start describing your business project – a simple explanation of the business, short enough to be delivered orally in the time taken to travel in a lift. Practise communicating your vision with confidence, clarity and transparency. Be prepared to answer the obvious questions people will ask – and don't be afraid to say, 'I don't know, but I will find out and come back to you' when that is the most truthful answer. If your request for funds is met with a 'No', ask why. The feedback you receive may enable you to make winning adjustments to your plans and your presentation for the next time round.

If at all possible, strive to diversify your sources of funding. That is, avoid relying on one or two individuals to support your business – if your chief 'angel' decides to back out or is unable to participate, your entire plan may collapse. If, instead, you attract equal investments from, say, 10 individuals, then you will be able to survive two or three losses without being badly affected.

Above all, remember that integrity is key to the success of any business – especially a small, entrepreneurial start-up. Lacking a history, a recognizable brand name, and a pre-existing customer base, your company is only as valuable as your word. Keep your promises, don't exaggerate, be transparent, and adhere to the highest possible values in all your dealings. In time, word will spread about the kind of business person you are – and a reputation for integrity will attract the best customers and partners to work with you – the kind you want to build your brand.

Raising funds for a new business has never been easy. In today's challenging financial climate, it's a little tougher than in the past, but the money is there for anyone with a genuinely worthwhile business idea, a strong commitment to success, and the leadership skills required to realize his or her vision. If you are personally dedicated to the entrepreneurial dream, go for it – and keep pushing!

A Spring filled with hope for all four seasons

The Arab Spring – with its social and economic disruptions, its political turmoil, its occasional descents into chaos and even violence – has served as an inescapable reminder of the many serious problems the Middle East faces. I've tried to address some of these challenges in this chapter, always mindful of the fact that many others with greater wisdom than I are working hard to resolve them.

It seems to me that, on balance, the Arab Spring has been a positive event. At the very least, it sent a reminder to leaders and citizens throughout the region that change is inevitable, and that we must plan for that change if we hope to guide it into positive, constructive and peaceful channels. Simply trying to keep the lid on the frustrations and anxieties of people – especially young people – in the hope that nothing will ever change is not a practical choice in the long run. It also reminds us that the voices of the people *will* be heard, even if those voices have gone unheeded for a long time – and that it's very risky for leaders to assume that those voices will always be on their side.

Fortunately, there are signs that the most far-sighted leaders in the region are paying close attention to the lessons of the Arab Spring, and are working hard to respond to the human needs those dissident voices express. The ideas I've proposed in this chapter are intended as a humble contribution to the healthy ongoing dialogue that the upheavals of recent years have stimulated.

As a corporate leader, I am naturally especially interested in the economic ramifications of today's social and political debates. For the most part, I'm not inclined to take sides. If pressed, I would say that I hope the region will gradually move in the direction of greater democracy – if by democracy we mean a governmental system that is institution-based, more flexible, open to change, and responsive to the preferences of the citizenry, inclusive of all constituents. I don't think this necessarily requires any specific constitutional structure, although constitutional changes may be appropriate in particular countries, depending on the wishes of the people and national circumstances. But I do believe that the long-term health of societies in the region requires an ability to make adjustments to societal trends through due process, and without any need for violent or abrupt regime change.

The basic challenge confronting the peoples of our region is about trying to strike an appropriate balance between change and stability, progress and tradition. As a society, we subscribe wholeheartedly to Islam as a guiding faith, without necessarily endorsing all of the varying interpretations that have emerged in recent years, some of which shy away from the essence of moderation. And for some, the desire to maintain our Islamic tradition leads to fear of change. They wonder: if we open up our societies to influences from the rest of the world, will we introduce values that are alien to us and beyond our ability to control? Because of this understandable anxiety, we've been slow to embrace change – perhaps too slow at times. We need to carefully adjust the balance so as to permit greater flexibility while avoiding dislocations that might be overwhelming and destabilizing of society as a whole.

In the near term, no one can predict precisely how the political and social changes transforming the region will turn out. Individuals and organizations who haven't played leadership roles in the past may rise to new positions of influence in particular countries, with results that may be good or bad. Over time, if governance systems are flexible and instil orderly transformation as a natural process in response to evolving circumstances, the long-term trends should be positive.

I'm especially hopeful that the Arab Spring will ultimately usher in a new era of economic opportunity. As I suggested at the start of this chapter, the impetus behind the entire movement was largely economic – the understandable desire of millions of young men and women for greater opportunities to work, create new wealth, and contribute to building the society of the future. If society responds appropriately, it could result in a generation of young people becoming more fully integrated into the economy as responsible employees, civil servants and entrepreneurs.

This new wave of wealth creation will lead to a healthier, more sustainable economy than the old system, where wealth often tended to remain in the hands of a fortunate few (the so-called '1 per cent'). The goal should be a system where the distribution of wealth is a constant process, like the recycling of water, ever flowing and circulating its benefits throughout all layers of society. With wealth distributed among the entire population, the prospects for economic growth will be enormous. Think about it this way: when people who are already wealthy add still more to their bank account, the impact on society is small. Once you own several houses, a fleet of cars, and wardrobes full of clothing, how much more can you buy?

By contrast, when people who are at the lower end of the economic scale join the middle class – or when people who are barely of middle-class status increase their income to become more comfortable – their spending increases dramatically. They and their families can now enjoy many more of the basic products whose production and sale largely drive economic growth – food, household items, health and beauty supplies, and other 'comfort products' that make daily life more pleasant and enjoyable. Over time, larger purchases become possible. The newly middle-class family is able to buy a new car, a set of nice appliances for the kitchen, and well-made clothing. Their children may be able to attend college. Multiply the effect by a few million people, and you have factories booming, thousands of jobs being created, and entire industries flourishing – along with the communities that house them.

This is why most of the great economic booms of history have been built on an expanding middle class – not further enrichment of the wealthy. And that is why the democratic, inclusive spirit of the Arab Spring points towards the best long-term direction for building thriving economies around the Middle East.

The stirrings of change symbolized by the Arab Spring make me feel optimistic about the future. I look forward to a day when the Middle East and North Africa form a single economic region in which expanding businesses are able to serve a vast land mass filled with a growing, increasingly prosperous population overflowing with opportunity. Imagine the MENA countries as a unified region with consistent, streamlined bureaucracy, an efficient, interconnected logistical and transportation infrastructure, enhanced by a common language that facilitates communication, travel and trade. It's an inspiring vision that I hope and believe will come true within the lifetime of today's youth.

HISHAM EZZ AL-ARAB
A banker's integrity at work

Fortunately, the MENA region is already blessed with many outstanding leaders who are demonstrating, by example, the kinds of qualities we need to encourage in the leaders of the future. I've profiled some of them in this book, and now I'd like to share the story of yet another such Unknown Leader – Hisham Ezz Al-Arab, one of the leading bankers in the Middle East, who has helped to transform and modernize the entire banking industry in Egypt.

I met Hisham in the mid-1990s when B.I.G. embarked on an expansion programme into Egypt. Our plan was to build a new speciality chemicals facility in the country, taking advantage of skilled local labour and selling into the large, prosperous Egyptian market. As with any major expansion, it raised the question: what bank should we choose to help smooth our entry into this new arena?

The name we heard over and over again as the most business-friendly bank was Cairo's Commercial International Bank (CIB), the leading financial institution in the country. They did a fine job of working with us on our entry into Egypt, and within a few years Hisham had taken over the bank. He was young and full of energy, and radiated a leadership style that combined the best qualities of modern banking with the deepest values and principles of a traditional banker. While high-level global banking and humility don't always go hand in hand, I found in Hisham a man of true humility – a straight shooter whose integrity was spotless.

Hisham was also a dedicated problem solver. In the early 2000s, when a financial crisis made it difficult to obtain vital access to the hard currency we needed to purchase raw materials for our Egyptian operation, Hisham went out of his way, drawing on the bank's vast resources, to ensure personally that we could conduct business without a single interruption.

Finally, Hisham has always been a source of invaluable business counsel. Whenever I visit Cairo, I make a point of having breakfast or lunch with him to get an informal briefing on the local economic climate. Half an hour of advice from Hisham is worth more than a dozen white papers by respected economic gurus. His recommendations are always absolutely impartial – as when he wisely advised me against making a business acquisition, despite the fact that handling the deal would have generated handsome fees for his bank. Later on, we realized how insightful his advice had been.

Hisham Ezz Al-Arab, in many ways, represents the kind of ideal business leader we need to replicate by the hundreds or thousands as the region grows in wealth, influence and stature. This fact alone makes his story worth sharing with anyone who aspires to belong to the next generation of leaders.

For many people, what turns out to be the ideal career is *not* their first or even their second job out of university. Sometimes it takes a significant period of experience, learning and growth – with a heavy dose of self-reflection – to discover the perfect way to express and make the most of your peculiar talents.

Hisham Ezz Al-Arab had a clear idea of the career path he wanted to follow after university. He wanted to work in the hospitality business, perhaps running a hotel or helping to manage a chain of such properties. He had spent three consecutive summers working at a fine hotel in the very shadow of the pyramids, and after graduation he was offered a job there. However, Hisham's father had a different idea – he thought his son would achieve greater success in banking, and he even arranged for a job offer through a friend who worked at a bank.

Young Hisham took an extreme step to help him decide which path to follow: he actually accepted *both* jobs, and worked in both places for a month! He spent mornings and afternoons at the bank, and then worked a full night shift in the front office of the hotel.

Hisham recalls those days as being 'exhausting but fun'. In the end, he discovered that he enjoyed the creative challenge and international flavour of banking even more than hospitality, and so he followed that career path.

The lesson: don't allow your mind to be quickly closed against alternative choices. Sometimes the road you were meant to follow takes time to discover.

Another incident from an early stage in Hisham's career offers a different, but equally important, lesson for life. Adopting the attitude of a lifelong learner is one way to avoid one of the most common, and serious, mistakes in business – the readiness to accept the common wisdom at face value, to assume that 'what everybody says' must be the truth. If you make it your business never to make this assumption, but instead to *find out for yourself* what is happening in the real world, you'll often be one step ahead of your rivals in business – and sometimes several steps.

A classic illustration of this truth comes from a story that Hisham Ezz Al-Arab likes to tell about the late Rodney B Wagner, a former vice-chairman of JP Morgan who was a friend and mentor of Hisham's during his years of learning about investment banking. Wagner was JP Morgan's director of credit in the Middle East in the years (up until 1979) when Shah Mohammad Reza Pahlavi was in power in Iran. During this time, many of Wagner's colleagues at the bank urged him to approve loans to the Iranian regime. 'Other banks are doing business with Iran', they said. 'There is a lot of money to be made there.'

Wagner disagreed. He sensed that the country was unstable, and he wasn't sure that the Shah's regime would be able to repay the money. But his colleagues said, 'You should visit Iran with us. You'll see that the country is in good shape, and you'll realize that the risks you worry about are false.'

Finally, Wagner went along on a visit to Tehran. He and his colleagues participated in several days of briefings and presentations by government officials, as well as conversations with business leaders and economists who received the stamp of approval from the Shah's regime. They toured selected factories and neighbourhoods under the guidance of government escorts. They saw a prosperous country filled with happy people who praised the Shah and were optimistic about the future.

However, Wagner wasn't satisfied. On the last day of the trip, while his colleagues relaxed with books by the hotel swimming pool, he decided to learn a little more about Iran by looking at it from a perspective other than the official one. He walked into the streets of Tehran, hailed a taxi, and said to the driver, 'I'll pay you for your work for a full day. Please take me to see the real Iran.'

The driver took Wagner all over the city. They visited poor neighbourhoods where Wagner talked to unemployed people; they went into slums where children were barefoot and had no schools to go to; they even went to the driver's own home, met his family and friends, talked about their lives, and had lunch together. By the end of the day, Wagner understood more about daily life among ordinary people in Iran than his colleagues who'd stayed by the hotel pool.

Back in New York City, after his colleagues had heaped praise on the Shah's regime and the economic future of Iran, Wagner chimed in. 'You guys haven't seen Iran', he said. 'I have. The country is poor. The people are suffering, and many of them are angry. This country is a volcano, ready to erupt.' Wagner stuck to his previous conviction that lending money to Iran would be a mistake.

Six months later, the Iranian revolution happened. For several days after that, Wagner's colleagues who'd criticized him for being 'too timid' to invest in Iran were unable to look him in the eye.

We're not prescribing a political view here. The point of this story is simply to illustrate the importance of assessing a situation from all angles and from the ground up as a source of learning and decision-making. And of course, there are times when the conventional wisdom is correct, and it would be just as foolish to base a decision purely on one city tour as it would be to avoid doing first-hand research altogether. But numbers alone – important as they are – can't tell you the whole story about a business decision. The numbers must be complemented by a ground-view level of what is happening. When you take the time to examine a situation in person, you develop the knowledge that enables you to connect the dots, develop independent judgement, and stop assuming that 'what everybody knows' must be true.

Having mastered the art of banking at JP Morgan, Hisham moved to Cairo to join CIB in 1999, taking over as chairman and managing director in 2002. He rapidly modernized the company, leading the creation and implementation of a new information infrastructure, improving the training of employees and managers, and introducing new decision-making protocols that enhanced the efficiency, productivity and profitability of the bank. These changes spearheaded improvements in the entire banking sector that helped catapult Egyptian finance into the 21st century.

Hisham also instilled in his organization a strong sense of leadership based, in the first instance, on absolute integrity:

> *Leadership always starts with myself. This has a very concrete meaning. Suppose there's a need to cut costs at the bank. Perhaps I will decide it's important to get the people to turn the lights off when they leave in order to trim unnecessary expenses. If so, the most important thing for me to do is turn the light off in my office before I walk out. In the same way, if I have a credit card I've been given by the bank, I have to be strict about using it only for bank purposes, never for my own – otherwise, how can I tell my people not to use a bank credit card for their personal use? Or if I tell my driver at the end of a work day, 'Leave the car for me because I'm going out with my friends tonight', how can I discipline other employees for misusing bank property?*

As Hisham's examples remind us, you can't lead without authenticity. If your actions fit your words, then your words will have meaning to others. But if the two don't match, your words will be hollow and are likely to be ignored – deservedly so.

Faith is an important source of Hisham's authenticity. He expresses it this way:

To consistently make the right decision as to how to behave in business, I think you have to be a believer. If you believe there is a supreme being out there called God who is watching you, you're going to pick the right decisions. You could rely on your own judgement, but, if you think there is a greater power watching you, you know you cannot outsmart him; you'll always think about it when you make decisions, either in business or in life. This belief helps keep you on the right path.

Today, Hisham is justly proud of the spirit among employees at CIB, as revealed by their behaviour during one of the most difficult times any business person can recall – the political, social and business upheaval in Egypt during the tumultuous year of 2011. Hisham says:

I'm proud to report that we recently received 17 awards from six different institutions, many of them based on one thing – how we managed our business and preserved our shareholders' capital during the crisis of the past year. In a time when other institutions were faltering, we managed to strengthen the bank's position. This achievement was possible because of the culture we've created and the fact that the people who work here truly love and care about the organization.

Awards don't tell the whole story of what makes CIB special. An even better indicator is some of the behaviour that Hisham observed first-hand:

When you see a bank officer who lives close to a branch office that is not the one he works at, and who takes it upon himself to go and help guard that branch during the days of revolution in the streets, putting his own life at risk, you have to respect that. When you see bank employees making special security arrangements to bring corporate customers to our central vault during periods of curfew when all banks are shut, so they can receive the money their companies need to make payroll, that's a remarkable thing. And when every bank manager, during a period when cell phone and e-mail systems have been shut down across the country, takes it upon himself to personally conduct a daily headcount of all employees to make sure that everyone is safe and sound, that says something special about the people at CIB.

Hisham is a modest man – it is one of the qualities that makes him an outstanding leader. He would never claim the credit for having created the remarkable spirit of cooperation, caring and courage that pervades CIB – and it's only right to give full recognition to the very special men and women who make up the bank staff, and who gave so fully of themselves during difficult times. But it's also fair to say that, without the inspiring leadership of Hisham Ezz Al-Arab, it's unlikely that CIB could have attracted and nurtured such a dedicated team of employees.

The Arab Spring has been a time of questioning, when leaders in every kind of institution are being challenged to look deeply within themselves and their organizations, asking whether they are doing all they can to build the dynamic future the people deserve and demand. Unknown Leaders like Hisham Ezz Al-Arab represent some of the best that the region has to offer, and a model of the kind of leadership that will guide us toward a brighter tomorrow.

Tomorrow belongs to you – so don't let go!

As you can see, the future I am envisioning for the MENA region is more varied, less hierarchical and more open than its past. Those accustomed to wealth and power should embrace the idea of sharing them with a wider array of their fellow citizens, because it ultimately leads to nation-building at its best. As Europe and North America have shown, it's possible for openness and debate to coexist with prosperity, innovation, growth and vitality – and I'm convinced they can also coexist with a lasting commitment to the values that have made the region a source of learning and knowledge for centuries.

If you are one of the millions of young people in the region who are wondering about the future, perhaps excited by the energies unleashed in the Arab Spring, but uncertain as to what they portend for our societies, I hope you will resolve to apply your own leadership talents to building the kind of entrepreneurial economy I've described. Creating such a meritocratic, dynamic, flexible society will not be easy, and it won't happen overnight. There will be frustrations and setbacks along the way. But the tides of history are flowing in the right direction, and the enormous innate talents of the region's people will surely drive enormous progress in the decades to come.

It's easy to fall into attitudes of cynicism: 'Why bother to work hard? The system is rigged. There's no place for someone like me', and so on. But cynicism doesn't lead to success. Don't wait around for a fairer, more open society to emerge by magic. Instead, start working today to help create that society! Apply your talents to whatever excites, inspires and motivates you. Create value for yourself and the people around you. Build a new business, a non-profit organization, a school or health care provider, or any other kind of institution that can help to meet our society's needs. Yes, it will take time and lots of hard work to reach your goals – but the person who starts the race today has the edge over those who remain on the sidelines, complaining.

The Arab Spring is all about making the world a better place, but that doesn't refer only to political or social transformation. Remember, you make the world a better place whenever you excel at what you do, regardless of what it may be. A farmer cultivating a small field of crops, a teacher instructing a class full of 10-year-olds, a shopkeeper running a small store on a city corner – if these individuals do a great job, they are all providing goods and services that will make life better for somebody else. Whatever your work is and no matter how simple or complex, always execute it with excellence, and never allow yourself to settle for mediocrity. When we accept mediocrity as individuals, the result is mediocre organizations and ultimately a mediocre society. If this were to happen to the region, it would be a betrayal of the bright promise of the Arab Spring, the many sacrifices behind it, and the pure meaning it stands for.

No one can predict the future with certainty, although I am optimistic about what the future holds for the peoples of the Middle East. But one thing seems certain: as our societies transform, we as individuals must transform as well. As the region continues to grow and diversify, both in demographic and in economic terms, true leaders will be in greater demand than ever, especially leaders who evolve as the world around them changes – in other words, practitioners of 'leadership in motion'.

I hope this book has encouraged you to nurture that quality in yourself and to encourage its growth in those around you. It is the leaders of tomorrow who will make our world a better place, both for us and for generations yet unborn.

Epilogue: tribute to Unknown Leaders everywhere

A tribute is the grateful recognition we offer to those who sacrifice something of themselves for the good of others, expecting neither reciprocation nor reward. For example, societies pay tribute to the Unknown Soldiers who gave their country the most precious gift – the gift of life itself. Their names are lost to history, but we recognize and honour them because they made this selfless sacrifice to benefit all of us.

No sacrifice can compare to the offering of one's life on the battle-field in order to protect and preserve one's homeland and its way of life. But over the years I've come to appreciate another group of extraordinary individuals who also deserve our recognition and gratitude. The Unknown Leaders offer their society something different from what the Unknown Soldiers have given, and though it is less dramatic than the gift of military heroism it is precious and remarkable in its own right.

In their everyday work in all walks of life, the Unknown Leaders give more of themselves to others and expect less in return. They end each day with society owing them a bit more – although they themselves believe that society owes them nothing beyond the opportunity to continue to give selflessly, without ceasing. Their contributions are like countless rivers and streams of all shapes, speeds and sounds that flow into one another and ultimately find their way to the ocean, feeding and enriching the entire society, especially the aspirations and dreams of the young people.

In the process of researching and writing this book, I've been privileged to learn more about Unknown Leaders than I ever knew before. I've studied what makes them tick, how they develop their skills and personal qualities, and the ethical values that make them admirable models of integrity and wisdom.

I've also had the opportunity to explore the career experiences of more than a dozen of these remarkable individuals, whom I've had the privilege to know up close. Their stories, observations and advice appear throughout these pages. I hope you enjoyed meeting these special people as much as I enjoyed sharing their stories with you.

Like other special people, Unknown Leaders are impossible to pigeonhole. Each one is unique and occupies a personal niche that no one else could fill. But they have a number of traits in common that help to define what makes them invaluable contributors to our world.

Unknown Leaders:

- give more than they take;

- don't seek recognition, praise or fame, but rather the self-fulfilment that comes from the consciousness of a job well done;

- are humble and modest, quick to praise others and to share the credit for accomplishments with all those who deserve it;

- refuse to participate in or surrender to the negativity that so many people wallow in;

- help make our world a place of hope and high achievement;

- can be found almost everywhere – in business, at home, in school, in government, in the non-profit sector, in professional work, in hospitals and clinics, and in companies and organizations large and small;

- have earned our encouragement, support and honour, along with ever-expanding opportunities to grow and lead;

- are needed today in greater numbers than ever.

Feet on the ground, head held high (but *not* lost in the clouds) and heart in the right place – that, in a nutshell, is my portrait of the Unknown Leader! In my own life and work, I hope to live up to that image, but if I fail at least I'll try my utmost, every day – and, in the end, that consistent effort is what truly matters.

Leadership, I've discovered, begins in the heart and mind of a single person. Its seeds are sown through a journey of self-discovery; it grows and develops through years of introspection, self-questioning, experimentation and a rigorous effort. In time, this inner quality of leadership can shape and uplift an entire organization – and some-times a whole nation.

The six qualities I've described in this book can be found in all great leaders. Of course, there are variations in these qualities among different kinds of leaders and in different situations. Great leaders may exhibit these qualities to varying degrees and in varying ways. If you aspire to the ranks of leadership, you need to accept the chal-lenge of developing all six qualities in yourself – every day, with every action you take and every decision you make.

The journey of self-development is at times agonizing, and there are no guarantees as to the outcome, yet when we take the high road and stay on it the feeling is indescribably gratifying. In an ironic way, we feel more natural, more our true self and more in touch than ever before – as well as a strong sense of humility. We become better people, better spouses, better parents and better colleagues. What's more, we possess the fabric and makings of genuine leadership.

Our guide and compass along this journey is our faith – our faith in ourselves, our faith in the almighty Creator, and our faith in the fact that we are in our present position for a bigger reason and a larger good.

Regardless of the outcome, this journey is a prize in itself whether we do evolve into the leader we wish to be or not. Others close to us will see a remarkable difference in what we have become. This voyage into one's self is an uplifting course, though demanding, and one that calls for personal courage and resilience. Since this is a lifetime journey, there is no finish line and no stop signs. We just keep raising the bar at our own pace. More importantly, we'll leave behind a legacy that enriches the people we've touched, the organizations we've strengthened and the causes we've championed.

But let us not allow the mind with its fears, its doubts and its on-and-off tricks to hold us back from experiencing the ride of a lifetime.

As the MENA region evolves and grows into an ever-expanding role on the world stage, leadership at every level becomes more and more important. Of course, we need leaders in corporate boardrooms and in government offices, but we also need them on factory floors, in high schools and colleges, in hospitals and clinics, in every small business and retail store, in our everyday workplace, and even in our homes and families.

As you've seen in this book, there are many Unknown Leaders already doing heroic work in these places today, but many more are needed for the greater challenges we face tomorrow.

Consider this book a formal invitation to welcome you into the club of Unknown Leaders! It's a very special group of people: unassuming, but remarkably instrumental. As a member of this vast, humble but exclusive club, you'll find that life is a never-ending series of fascinating challenges and opportunities – an epic journey that is a personal triumph in itself, worthy of an 'Unknown Leader'.

So start your journey, stay the course – and have a story worthy of telling!

About the author

Global visionary – whether leading a successful business or setting a course for academic pursuits, Sheikh Hussein A Al-Banawi is a man of vision. When he chose to cross the world to attend Rollins College in Winterpark, Florida, the native Saudi Arabian had three criteria in making his decision. First, Hussein A Al-Banawi preferred to be in a southern climate, having received his associate of arts degree in Switzerland. Second, he wanted to attend a small, high-quality institution. And finally – and perhaps the most unique requirement – he wanted a place where no Arab students had preceded him. His vision, he explained, was to pioneer a positive image and connection to the West. 'And I hope I did a fair job,' Al-Banawi said. 'That's something my successors can determine… those who came after me as students from the Arab world.'

After graduation, Al-Banawi returned to Jeddah, Saudi Arabia, and his new role first as division president, then as president and CEO into the present time as chairman and CEO of the Banawi Industrial Group (B.I.G.), a market leader in specialty chemicals, packaging and food flavours in the Broader MENA (Middle East and Africa) region since 1957, bringing with him new concepts for Middle Eastern business practices. He has been at the helm of the family business ever since, successfully guiding B.I.G. through an era of globalization and massive changes in technology. Creating a performance-driven corporate culture that focuses on customer satisfaction while enhancing shareowner value has been the key to keeping the business thriving in the midst of change, Al-Banawi has found.

As he looks to the future, Al-Banawi sees two challenges facing the Arab business world as it continues to seek growth opportunities. 'One is the ability for us to continue to provide the right education for future generations, because business is first and foremost about people,' he says. The second is being in an area that historically has had its fair share of political turmoil. The remedy to this, he believes, is continuing to engage internationally.

Al-Banawi did his undergraduate studies at Franklin College in Lugano, Switzerland, and holds a Masters in Business Administration from Rollins College. The melding of his business acumen and interest in academia led Al-Banawi to establish a Chair in Islamic Economics, Finance and Management at Rice University, his younger brother's alma mater. He sees the chair as a way of showing gratitude to the country that gave him the opportunity for higher education as well as a means for American and International students to examine past contributions of the Arab civilization to the science of economics in order to help solve today's complex economic issues. 'A lot of dust has settled on this science over many years, but maybe the world can take a look at it again, in today's terms, and perhaps adjust for the future,' Al-Banawi says. 'Over the years, academia has proved to be the right home for such initiatives.' He hopes to help launch future programmes that will bring MBA students into closer dialogue with business executives internationally.

Commenting on the importance of maintaining a balance between fast-paced business enterprise and the slower-paced cultural change through academia, Al-Banawi says, 'As human beings, it is God's gift that we have a pair of eyes. One has to be on today, and one has to be on tomorrow.'

Hussein A Al-Banawi is a member of the Board of Trustees, Vice Chairman of the Executive Committee and Chairman of the Investment Committee of the World Waqf Foundation of the Islamic Development Bank, and a founding member of The John D Gerhart Center for Philanthropy and Civic Engagement at The American University in Cairo.

Acknowledgements

For me, acknowledgements alone do not suffice to express my gratitude to those unique individuals who were behind my decision to become a first-time author. They cared so much and provided even more support throughout my expedition in writing *The Unknown Leader*.

Through it all, my beloved family, starting with my wife Majda, my daughters Liyan and Arwa, and my sons Hilal and Badr have been my constant source of comfort and support at home as I experienced the various stages of living and writing *The Unknown Leader*. They kept telling me, 'Dad, it's simple! You just need to share with others what you have shared with us over the years.' Their encouragement made it all possible.

My colleagues on the board of Banawi Industrial Group (B.I.G.) encouraged me from the start in a most simple but powerful way by telling me, 'Go ahead, what are you waiting for?' Their support went even further when my brother Waleed, one of our board members, was instrumental in identifying the talented writer who acted as my critic and adviser from start to finish. Waleed strongly felt that I owe it to young aspiring leaders to reach out to them through my book, and I am truly grateful for his belief in me and my mission.

I also want to thank Karl Weber, my editor and kick-the-tire writer. Before we got started on *The Unknown Leader*, I said, 'Karl, I intend to write my first book from scratch myself, but that doesn't mean

I can do this right without a first-class team member and a sounding board writer to keep me on message.' I couldn't have picked a better associate throughout this unique experience. Karl is truly gifted; he combines the demeanor of a buddy writer and the integrity of an honest critic. What made the time we spent feel like an unforgettable train ride through all the various stations, thinking out loud, exchanging views and putting the pieces together, was Karl's ability to see where I was going before I got there. This is Karl's secret.

And how about my friend Hani Khoja, who kept talking to me about the book way before I got started, so that over time it felt real – like imagining the smell of that great pizza in the oven before rolling the dough.

My immense gratitude goes to my right-hand colleague and confidante, Nawrus Nejaim. This extraordinary young woman was my barometer for sense and sensibility as I plowed through countless trials for expressing myself. Nawrus is a natural; I can never forget her subtle head movement as a signal to me that said 'Something is missing here', or when she nodded in agreement to say 'You've hit the bull's eye with this one!' When I asked Nawrus to join B.I.G. as her first real job after college, she hesitated a bit until I offered her the chance to work with me on *The Unknown Leader*. That was the catch! And Nawrus surpassed the expectations of everyone who worked closely with her on the book project.

I also owe buckets of gratitude to so many more who genuinely felt that as an individual I was worthy of being an author and had a story worthy of telling. Topping that list are the outstanding men and women, the Unknown Leaders, whose stories give the readers a glimpse of their lifelong journey. The list includes: Dr May Al-Dabbagh, Sameer Al Ansari, Nabil Alyousuf, Dr Asma Siddiki, Hani Khoja, Dr Ghazi Binzagr, Dr Mahmoud El-Gamal, Dr Haifa Jamal Al-Leel, Moataz Al-Alfi, Hisham Ezz Al-Arab, Dr Waleed Bukhari, Maha Al-Ghunaim, and Dr Ebtisam Dkahkhni. Thanks to all of these distinguished individuals for their willingness to share their inspiring personal stories.

Finally, one last heartfelt acknowledgment goes to you, the reader, who took time to join me, one chapter after another. I hope that you have found reading *The Unknown Leader* worth your while. I would be even more appreciative to receive your feedback, so that if I am destined to have a second go at writing a book, I will be a better author next time.

Hussein A Al-Banawi
www.theunknownleader.com

Index